WHAT TO DO WHEN
YOU'RE THE
SPEAKER™

THE CATHCART
METHOD™
FOR CONFIDENT
COMMUNICATION

JIM CATHCART, CSP, CPAE
WITH JAN PAYNE

"I have known Jim Cathcart for a decade or longer. We first met when I was looking for insider advice from a top-level professional speaker. That inquiry resulted in a treasured friendship. If you can learn from Jim, do it! I certainly do"

Michael Reagan, author, speaker, and son of President Ronald Reagan

"You have something special. You have greatness in you. I strongly recommend this book by Jim Cathcart. This is "the Bible" for this industry! If you're serious about learning how to present with confidence, this book is a masterpiece."

Les Brown, inspirational speaker, author and success guru

"Jim Cathcart is one of the most intelligent and entertaining speakers in America, and in the world today. He has been a guide and an inspiration to me personally for more than thirty years."

Brian Tracy, speaker/author/thought leader

"Behind every world class performer there is a world class mentor. Jim Cathcart is the best in making what you are telling..compelling!"

Denis Waitley, author *The Psychology of Winning*

"I've known and admired Jim Cathcart since the late 1970s when we were both aspiring speakers growing our careers. We have served together on boards and committees, shared social times and business collaborations. Through it all I have found Jim to be a man of character and a compelling speaker. We invited him to serve as Artist in Residence at High Point University. That should tell you that Jim is a speaker you can trust to bring great ideas to your organization."

Dr. Nido R. Qubein, President, High Point University

"Jim Cathcart and I have been colleagues and close friends for over 40 years. I've seen him captivate and inspire audiences all over the country.
You will do very well to study the wisdom of this world-class speaker."

Don Hutson, Hall of Fame Speaker, and co-author of the #1 New York Times/Wall Street Journal Best-Seller, The One Minute Entrepreneur

"Having known and worked with Jim for decades, I have always admired his desire to go above and beyond to ensure everyone involved in an event has a positive experience. Jim's humble approach to providing service as a professional speaker is what has created the tremendous, long-term success he has enjoyed. Take his wisdom to heart, follow in his footsteps, and you, too, will enjoy great success as a speaker."

Tom Hopkins, The Builder of Sales Champions, author of When Buyers Say No

"For years now I have been aware of Jim Cathcart as a speaker. Recently I have also come to know him as a neighbor and a friend. If he gives you speaking advice, I suggest you take it!"

Dr. Ivan Misner NY Times Bestselling Author and Founder of BNI

"There's no one better to have in your corner than Jim Cathcart when it comes to a speaking coach. Jim's ideas are framed with significance and wisdom. From novice to expert speaker, this is a must-read book."

Steve Spangler, STEM Educator | Television Host DIY Sci, Speaking Hall of Fame Inductee

"Jim Cathcart started his speaking business in 1977. There is a reason he's thrived in the industry and is recognized as one of best. Because he is. His talent on stage, combined with his ability to successfully run a speaking business for so many years, in good times and bad, is no small feat. He's a master at every facet of the business. And now he shares his wisdom with you!"

Shep Hyken, award-winning keynote speaker and New York Times bestselling author

"Jim Cathcart is a pioneer in the speaking industry. He has decades of wisdom from wowing audiences around the world."

Jason Dorsey, global speaker and bestselling author of Zconomy

"The ONE book you must read whether you're a veteran speaker or just starting out! Jim Cathcart breaks down every element of the speaking process from preparing to speak to receiving feedback in a way you can learn from quickly. You will find yourself using it at as your speaking reference guide for years to come."

Mark Hunter, CSP, "The Sales Hunter"
author of High-Profit Selling

"It is said that for those who have enjoyed a large measure of success in their career, it's important to send the elevator back down. Jim Cathcart has spent his career lifting aspiring speakers with his decades of excellence and eloquence from the stage. This book is your opportunity to sit at the feet of a master. Don't let it pass you by! Go make yourself a cup of coffee, grab a highlighter and take years off your learning curve."

David Avrin, CSP, Global Speaking Fellow
Keynote Speaker, Author, Consultant, Podcast Host

"Jim Cathcart is one of my all-time favorite heroes. I've known Jim and his exceptional work as a speaker, writer, coach and consultant for decades.
No question, Jim is one of the most inspiring and influential speakers in the world. His depth and breadth of knowledge truly brings out the best in his audiences. Jim challenges you to think and better yet gives you the tools and motivation to act. "

Niki McCuistion, Executive Producer/Pres & CEO
McCuistion Perspectives TV Program

"I've been helping professional speakers get onto stages for over 20 years, and I wish I could have given every one of them a copy of this book.
It WILL make you a better presenter."

Dave Reed, co-founder of eSpeakers.com
and non-profit Speak For Good

"*Working with Jim Cathcart has been a life-changing experience for me. His guidance and mentorship have not only boosted my speaking confidence, but also helped me grow personally and professionally. Jim has a natural charisma that makes you feel like you're in the presence of someone truly special. He's the epitome of professionalism, and his dedication to his craft is truly inspiring. In my opinion, working with Jim is the best investment you can make for yourself. He's a rare gem in the industry, and his expertise is unmatched. If you're looking for a mentor who will challenge you to be your best and push you to new heights, Jim Cathcart is the perfect choice.*"

Kate Hancock, Hancock + Robbins Co. Harvard Business School Web3 Thought Leader. Top 100 Women of the Future. 2X INC 5000 list Awardee. Serial Entrepreneur.

"*This book teaches you how to be well-prepared, perform at your peak, and deal calmly with the unexpected. Jim's advice on using humor has made my speaker introductions and speech content more lighthearted, which has helped me connect with my audience.*"

Jodi Rifkin, M.A. Ed., DTM, E-Commerce Thought Leader and Kaizen Strategist

"*Jim Cathcart is a legendary speaker not only because of the impact of his presentations but because of his heart's desire to help others become better in every area of their life. Jim truly shows up 100% for the benefit of the audience. I wish this book was available 15 years ago when I started my speaking journey. The wisdom and practical tips on speaking in this book are essential for every speaker of any level of experience.*"

Tom Ziglar, CEO of Zig Ziglar Corporation, speaker and author

"*As an introvert, I never thought I'd become an award-winning speaker. My secret to success has been learning best practices, then repeating those practices every time. That's why I love Jim's book; it cuts the learning curve in half. It breaks down, step-by-step, every best practice you need in order to master the stage and the room.*"

Matthew Pollard, The Rapid Growth Coach, Bestselling Author of The Introvert's Edge Series

"*Who better than Jim Cathcart to teach public speaking? Seriously. He's literally in the Speakers' Hall of Fame. And more than any other speaking coach, his book will impact your speaking content in ways that other coaches can't. Just watch his videos. It's more than his polish in speaking. He teaches you how to emotionally connect with your audience relative to your important message. People buy on emotion. Jim is a genius.*"

John Mitchell, Founder of Think it Be it,
the man who uncovered the full secret of Think & Grow Rich

"*To learn the real secrets to success as a fantastic communicator is vitally important... to learn the true secrets from the one and only Jim Cathcart is PRICELESS! Look no further, grab this book, devour it, and then go to the nearest mirror and high five yourself for making such a great and awesome decision!*"

Erik "Mr. Awesome" Swanson, Multi #1 International
Bestselling Author & Award-Winning Speaker

"*This book is not just for professional speakers. The truth is, that we are ALL speakers every day. Therefore, this book is for you. I have been presenting publicly in one capacity or another for almost 40 years. I wish I had this book when I started!*"

Howard Partridge, International Business Coach
Phenomenal Business Coaching Powered by Zig Ziglar

"*This is a guide that helps seasoned speakers, as well as those who are just getting started. This is particularly good if you've got a presentation coming up and you want to make sure that you're ready for all possible scenarios. Don't try to do it alone or without the necessary knowledge. Read this book and you will gain the confidence and the skills needed.*"

Terry Brock, MBA, CSP, CPAE, CVP, Member,
Professional Speaker Hall of Fame

"This book is a goldmine of practical advice, insider tips, and inspiring stories that will help you cut years off your learning curve and take your speaking to the next level. Jim Cathcart is the "real deal" in speaking and in the business of speaking. His experience, wisdom, and generosity shine through every page of this book. Get this book, read it, and apply its lessons. You won't regret it!"

Tim Gard CSP, CPAE, Hall of Fame Speaker, expert Humorist

"There are many resources on delivering a better speech, but my great friend Jim Cathcart has written the Bible on how to be a distinctive speaker. There's an enormous difference between the two. Jim not only teaches how your presentation can make a greater impact on your audience, he gives you every conceivable nuance on each step you must take – on and off the platform – to stand out when you stand up to speak."

Scott McKain, CEO, The Distinction Institute; author of "The Ultimate Customer Experience" and "Iconic"

Hall of Fame Speaker, Jim Cathcart, has been at the top of the Speaking Business for decades. With the speaking industry about to explode from a two-billion-dollar-a-year industry to ten billion globally over the next 10 years, **What To Do When You are The Speaker** is the MUST HAVE book for every business owner, CEO, and independent entrepreneur who wants to be on the front end of this speaking explosion! Grab copies not just for yourself but for your clients, vendors, customers and entire team!

Michael D. Butler, CEO, Beyond Publishing

DEDICATION:

"I gratefully dedicate this book to the National Speakers Association, my professional family and cherished colleagues. It's because of you that I've been able to become a successful speaker and author.

I joined NSA in 1976 as an aspiring speaker. My business was just forming, and NSA only had around 200 members. Those members became not only my colleagues and mentors but also my friends.

As NSA grew to mold a new profession, it has had an impact around the globe on people like me who want to make a positive difference in the world.
Thank you to all who have worked to shape NSA and the speaking profession into the force for good that it has become.

Jim Cathcart, CSP, CPAE
NSA President 1988-89
Cavett Award Recipient 1993
Speaker Hall of Fame 1985
Certified Speaking Professional 1981

ISBN Hardcover: 978-1-63792-563-8
ISBN Softcover: 978-1-63792-564-5

FOREWORD

by Patricia Fripp, CSP, CPAE

In the world of professional speaking, few names stand as tall and as respected as that of Jim Cathcart. A true master of the craft, Jim has spent decades honing his skills, captivating audiences, and sharing his wisdom with aspiring speakers. That's why I'm thrilled to introduce you to this rare and invaluable book, *What To Do When You're The Speaker*™: *The Cathcart Method*™."

Jim and I first met at the National Speakers Association at the beginning of our careers, and I have seen-up-close-and-personal Jim's skill and wisdom grow.

There have been many books written about public speaking. I have written a couple myself! Believe me, this book is not just another collection of tips and tricks for public speaking. It is a comprehensive guide that delves deep into the art and science of effective communication. From the moment you step on stage to the final bow, Jim shares his tried-and-true methods for delivering impactful and memorable presentations.

Section one of the book covers a wide range of topics that will help you build a solid foundation for your speaking career. Jim discusses everything from how to be natural on stage, to managing your first impression, to recovering from a bad introduction. Each chapter provides valuable insights and practical advice that will elevate your skills and instill confidence in your abilities as a speaker.

In section two, Jim delves into the finer points of storytelling, audience engagement, and managing unexpected situations. You'll learn how to use props effectively, work with translators, and handle technical issues that may arise during your speech. The knowledge and experience shared in these pages will prove invaluable as you navigate the challenging and rewarding world of public speaking.

Section three is dedicated to helping you grow as a speaker, both on and off the stage. Jim shares strategies for building your brand, expanding your reach, and working with industry professionals. He also provides guidance on mastering the art of online presentations and webinars, an increasingly important skill in today's digital world.

Jim Cathcart's method is a culmination of decades of experience, dedication, and passion for the art of speaking. His commitment to helping others unlock their potential as speakers is evident on every page of this book. As you immerse yourself in the wisdom and techniques shared here, you will see a transformation in your approach to public speaking, and your skills will grow exponentially.

As fellow Hall of Fame speakers and Past Presidents of the National Speakers Association (NSA), both Jim and I understand the power and responsibility that comes with standing in front of an audience. This book is a testament to Jim's unwavering dedication to the craft and his genuine desire to help others succeed.

Whether you're an aspiring speaker, a seasoned professional, or simply someone who wants to improve their communication skills, *What To Do When You're The Speaker™: The Cathcart Method™* is an essential resource that will serve you well throughout your journey.

There are two ways to learn to be a great speaker. From your own experience or, the better way, from other people's experience. If you want to know what to do when you are the speaker, there is nobody better to learn from than Jim Cathcart.

Patricia Fripp, CSP, CPAE

Hall of Fame Speaker, Past President of NSA,

Coauthor *Deliver Unforgettable Presentations*

TABLE OF CONTENTS

Contents of section two

Contents of section three

A SON'S PERSPECTIVE

Growing up as the only child of a professional speaker is a unique experience.

Instead of getting signatures from sports heroes, my signature book was filled with legends like Zig Ziglar. Instead of getting "time outs" when I misbehaved, I got hour-long lectures on making the right choices. I remember hitting my teenage years and rebelling against the whole idea of self- improvement. And a desire for public speaking? Never. "It must've skipped a generation," I would say.

And then I grew up… and got a job in Learning & Development which led to a career in Human Resources in luxury hospitality. Public speaking? Check. How to motivate a team? Check.

Emotional intelligence? Check. All required skills in my (now 25 year) career. Only, I didn't go to college for *those* topics.

I had no formal training prior that which was provided by my company.

And yet I progressed up the ladder in HR. I felt I had a natural knack for it and had fun every day.

One would think, "you can learn a lot living with an expert in communication, IF you pay attention." I'm here to tell you that you absorb tons even if you don't.

It was only when I started my own professional career that I discovered my success was due to the things I had learnt from my dad from the beginning. Those one-hour lectures stuck.

Thankfully they were delivered by a man who: a) loved people, b) was himself constantly learning and c) knew how to communicate.

I've seen him deliver keynote speeches to thousands, and I've seen him wax poetic at the dinner table. At every point, he's a great communicator. Full of confidence, purpose and love for his audience.

My parents tell me my dad travelled 240 days out of the year when I was a kid. I can't believe that.

I could swear he was always around. He tells me he placed a lot of importance on our connection, whether in person or over the phone. I felt it, and still feel it today.

I keep growing because he's in my life.

I hope this book resonates with you, and helps you achieve your goals.

Jim Cathcart, Jr.

INTRODUCTION

Everyone Is A Public Speaker Sometimes.

Whether we are a *good* public speaker is a separate issue.
But ALL of us do it.

Common "public" speaking includes:
- Talking with friends around a dinner table
- Interviews, online and on stage
- Audience comments and questions
- Discussing ideas in a committee
- Giving a report or statement at a board meeting
- Posing a toast at a wedding or special event
- Introducing someone else who will be speaking
- Leading a meeting in person or via video call
- Facilitating a discussion or brainstorming session
- Putting comments on a flip chart or whiteboard for a group
- Making announcements on a Public
- Address system
- Offering a blessing prayer at a family meal
- Serving on a panel or discussion
- Reciting a poem, performing a song, or reading a passage from a book
- Replying to a question from an instructor during a meeting
- Delivering a report or speech or telling a story
- Telling a joke to a group
- Giving directions to more than one person at once
- Selling goods at an expo table
- Asking a group to "please be seated, our program is about to begin"
- Playing Charades or word guessing games
- Telling others about your recent experience.

Need I go on? If you are addressing more than one person, then you are speaking in public.

Where the nerves come in is when we realize that we are the center of attention.

That is when we stop thinking about our message and our audience and start thinking about ourselves. Boom! That's when nervousness appears.

THE FEAR OF SPEAKING ISN'T REALLY ABOUT SPEAKING AT ALL. IT'S ABOUT JUDGMENT.

Picture yourself on stage being interviewed by a friend. You are seated, comfortable, and with someone you trust. You are speaking on a topic you know well, and you are not nervous. Now, take your friend off the stage, remove the chair, and go stand at a lectern. Talk about the same topic to the same group. Would you suddenly get nervous? Most people do. But, in reality, all that changed was the focus on you. Remember, this is not about you. It is about the value you can communicate to your audience.

WHAT IF I'M NOT A "PROFESSIONAL SPEAKER?"

That shouldn't keep you from speaking more professionally.

Most speakers don't earn a living through public speaking. But some do! And they earn a substantial living by doing what others fear or hate: addressing a group. This is a life skill that will increase your value and reach in any field.

Even if you never intend to speak for pay, learning from these amazing people will make you a better speaker and leader. The same would be true for a sport or art. Golf or music for example. If you want to become an excellent amateur, study the pros.

What makes Professional Speakers successful is their ability to lose themselves in service to their audience. They focus on the message and getting it across to others instead of on themselves as the ones delivering it.

Sure, they have practiced their delivery, gained coaching and feedback, watched recordings of themselves giving a speech, worked on their enunciation, accents, and timing. Spent hours thinking about their ideas. Like any top performer, they have taken every part of what they do seriously. But once they are on stage, they are focused on reaching the audience with the intended impact. That is why they are not nervous or self-conscious. Self-aware? Yes. Self-conscious, no.

Every major professional speaker has hired a speech coach at some point. I've personally paid tens of thousands to coaches at key points in my career and it has made a big difference in my performance. Colleagues have told me of hiring acting coaches, choreographers, storytelling coaches, voice coaches, media coaches and image consultants to help them become better on every level of public communication. It is also powerfully valuable to have a Mentor to help you think about your topic and yourself from a higher or deeper level. None of us is as good as we could be.

Just remember:

Everyone in your audience is wanting you to do well.

They aren't waiting to judge you.

They are waiting to benefit from what you have to say.

Give them what they want. Be a pro every time you speak.

WHO IS JIM CATHCART?

Among professional speakers Jim Cathcart is one of the best-known, most admired and influential people in the business. He joined the National Speakers Association (NSA) in 1976, when it only had 200 members, and he helped grow it to the world-wide presence and stature it enjoys today. Jim's involvement includes ten years on the board of directors, chair of most of the major committees and the conventions, serving as president in 1988-89, and serving a term on the board of the Global Speakers Federation. He is the man who crafted the Professional Competencies that are the backbone of professional education in NSA and the structure used for the Certified Speaking Professional, CSP designation. Mr. Cathcart has received virtually every major award in the world for professional speaking. The Cavett Award from NSA, the CPAE Speaker Hall of Fame award, the Golden Gavel Award from Toastmasters International, the Sales & Marketing Hall of Fame Award from Top Sales World in London, the Lifetime Achievement Award from NSA Los Angeles, the Legends of the Speaking Profession from VSR, and so many more. He was a 29-year member of the prestigious Speakers Roundtable mastermind alliance. His TEDx video "How to Believe in Yourself" has over 2.6 million views.

Jim Cathcart has delivered more than 3,400 highly paid speeches to millions of people around the world. Every state in the USA, every province of Canada (except the Yukon…so far), ten tours of Australia, speeches in South America, Europe and Asia. From 2015 to 2019 Jim toured China to 23 major cities, delivering 4- and 6-hour lectures through an interpreter, to hundreds of thousands of eager learners. He has written and published 25 books, with more to come, and created learning programs for many major publishers. He's a university professor and Entrepreneur in Residence at California Lutheran University's School of Management and received an honorary business degree in 2021 from High Point University. Since 2021, Mr. Cathcart has been cohosting a long-running television show based in Texas called "McCuistion: Perspectives Matter." He interviews world leaders about key topics of the day. As founder of The Experts Academy™, Jim trains people to become Certified

Professional Experts, CPE™s. He also hosts the Wisdom Parlor Podcast.

In summary, Jim Cathcart has delivered more speeches in more varied settings and received more rewards for doing so than almost any speaker you will ever meet. He is based in Austin, Texas, USA and is a Mentor to Experts and Entrepreneurs around the world.

HOW TO GET THE MOST BENEFIT FROM THIS BOOK

STEP ONE: See it done. Access Jim Cathcart's YouTube channel and watch Jim deliver a keynote speech. We especially recommend the 2001 Golden Gavel Award speech "All Leadership Begins With Self Leadership." Also watch some of Jim's most recent 2023+ speeches to compare then vs now. There are scores of videos of Jim Cathcart online and available for free viewing.

Things to Watch For

- Masterful use of humor
- Stories to drive home his points
- Connection with the audience
- Use of Voice inflections
- Making eye contact with every person in the audience
- Compensating for the distraction of the huge head table behind him
- Natural and relaxed onstage demeanor
- Responding to the introducer
- Showing the importance of embracing his message
- Showing respect to others in the room

This powerful speech combines all of the elements covered in the Master Speaker course Jim teaches.

STEP TWO: Think it through.

Review the 54 lessons

Public Speaking Mini-Lessons

We have chosen this format because you can easily browse. Much of this is never covered in other people's books on speaking. These lessons were created to be studied quickly and applied immediately or discussed by a group.

You may schedule these for one lesson a day or once a week or create training sessions around half a dozen lessons each time. The key is to space the learning over time and to discuss and then apply each of the lessons. These can be done as exercises in class or in actual speaking engagements. Take the time to review and apply each lesson.

Each lesson takes between 2 and 10 minutes to read. Most are around 3 minutes. Review one short lesson, discuss the ideas and then apply them on your own. You can combine several lessons into a full classroom session. There is no fixed order for you to review these lessons. Skip around as needed and learn at your own pace.

Video: "All Leadership Begins With Self-Leadership" is Jim Cathcart's Golden Gavel Award keynote presentation, delivered before 1,500 Toastmasters leaders at their International Convention when he received their highest award. 39 minutes of humor, inspiration, motivation and ideas to be a better leader of yourself and others. Available from *http://Cathcart.com.* (Yes it was long ago but it is a good example to study.) *Note: In 2022 Jim was invited back for the third time in 27 years (1995, 2001, 2022) as the Opening Ceremonies Keynote Speaker at the Toastmasters International Convention in Nashville.*

STEP THREE: Notice more. There's more to see.

After you've read this book, watch Jim's Golden Gavel Keynote once again. (Note: you can also do this with any major speaker, watch, reflect, then watch again.) You will pick up nuances and techniques that completely escaped your attention during the first viewing. It's a good idea to do this with other classic speeches by people you admire.

Make it you. Once you have seen Jim in action, studied the tips and suggestions, read the stories and then seen it done again, your consciousness will have been imprinted with a whole new way of looking at public communication. Let this be the tool that flips that switch in you.

See it done • Think it through • Notice more • Make it you

SECTION 1

LESSON 1

HOW TO BE NATURAL ON STAGE

"I really appreciated your sincerity!" That is the number one comment, I have received consistently, for over 40 years. People say that I'm natural, that I come across as genuine, it doesn't seem to be an act and it's not a puffed-up version of me. That is true, when I'm speaking I'm telling the audience the truth. I can truly relate to people in a way that's appropriate to the speech that I'm giving.

The way to be natural on stage is to manage your ***intent.*** It is not about your content. Anybody can deliver that same content. It's your ***intent*** that determines how your content is delivered. If your ***intent*** is to genuinely help people get the message, they'll realize it. When your ***intent*** is to respect them and to show them a way to incorporate a lot of these ideas into their own world, they will recognize that. They'll sense that you genuinely care.

Learn to cultivate a caring ***intent*** and it will change the way you deliver your content. Manage the ***intent,*** tell the truth and don't try to sugarcoat it. Just tell people the truth. Be courteous, be appropriate, be professional and tell them the truth. Be fallible. Be willing to acknowledge that you make mistakes. If something goes wrong (and it invariably will) - be willing to acknowledge that it went wrong and just get right on with your speech. It's easy to be natural.

People can detect the unnatural or artificial presentation and will not connect with you. They may even miss your message altogether. When you are natural on-stage people will trust you, listen and get your message.

LESSON 2

OPENING AND CLOSING

You don't need to memorize your entire speech but for the opening and closing know **exactly** what you want to say, **verbatim.** Both your open and close are critical to your success! When you enter the stage, be prepared! You never get a second chance to make a first impression. Visualize it! Internalize it! Practice it! You want to be confident as you step on stage and speak, (You don't have to deliver the opening and closing lines word-for-word but have them in your mind verbatim anyway).

The greatest moments of tension for the speaker are the moment that the he or she first gets to the platform and the moment when they're closing the speech and getting ready to leave. To make sure you get it right, know, in advance, what you're going to say and how you're going to say it. That way, if the situation changes and you've got a different idea, you can always improvise. Be prepared to be confident, to be effective, to be clear, and to be right on target with what you **intended** to do. Know **exactly, verbatim,** your wrap up. This is your chance to leave a lasting impression. Make sure you know what that is. Be emphatic!

WHAT DO YOU DO DURING YOUR INTRODUCTION

You're sitting in a meeting room and you're next. Somebody is standing up on the platform and reading your introduction. What you do during that time? A lot of people would say *'I just wait until it's my turn and I speak.'* No, no, no! You're a professional, you've got a responsibility here.

Before you speak:
- Uncross your legs
- Breathe
- Check:
    - Mindset
    - Mic
    - Lighting
    - Obstacles

Uncross your Legs

First, uncross your legs. Maybe it's not a big deal but it could be a very big deal. Uncross your legs so that you've got full circulation. Free circulation in your lower extremities is important so that when you stand up you won't stumble. That could be an awkward moment, right? Next, look at the distance between you and the spot where you're going to speak. Is there anything in the way? Are there any cords on the floor? Are there any obstacles you've got to go around? Be aware!

Breathe!

Also, breathe from the gut. Do some relaxed breathing. It's not very pretty from the observation point of view but it has a good effect on you. Just breathe from your gut and it will relax your diaphragm so that you can speak with a little bit more power when you first start to speak. Listen to your introducer while you're doing these few, little physical exercises; noticing the path to the stage, listen to what your introducer is saying because the introducer might blow the introduction. They might say something wrong or put in a fact that is not correct or get your name wrong or something. You might want to determine whether you're going to respond to that or just start giving your speech. In addition, you might want to thank the person for the great introduction.

Mindset!

Mindset is one of the most important preps. Get in the right mindset, the right mood, take a look around you. Begin cultivating a feeling of caring about your audience. If you don't really feel that you can be of value to them or that you respect and admire them, it will show in the way you speak. Thoughts travel faster than the sounds of your voice! Notice whether you're visible to them. When you're being introduced, a lot of the people in the audience are going to be looking at you. If you're sitting over to the side, instead of them looking at the stage and the introducer, a lot of them will be watching you. Pay attention to what messages you're conveying, even nonverbally, as you're sitting there.

Thomas Troward said- 'Scientists tell us our thoughts travel at 186,000 miles per second, which is 930,000 times faster than the sound of our voice.'

People are Watching You!

No need to be self-conscious about it, just be aware that other people are looking. If the introducer is saying something that sounds like an exaggeration, you might want to roll your eyes and smile, shake your head or do some kind of a little brushoff sort of the gesture or you might just want to sit there calmly and solemnly.

Is Your Mic On?

Is your microphone on? It is much better to find out off stage than when you reach the platform! Don't blow into it. Simply give it a little tap. That's enough, it will come through the sound system. You'll know whether your mic is on. If you're wearing a lavaliere (clip on) mic, that's especially true, you want to make sure you've turned it on. If it is a mic with a cord instead of a wireless, you want to make sure that the cord is plugged in fully and the cord is not hooked around something.

Lighting

Notice where the light is shining. When you walk to the stage, walk into the light. Walk to the spot where there's going to be full lighting on your face in your opening comments and your eye contact and your facial gestures can be seen by everybody in the audience. During the time that you're being introduced, notice all those things. Notice the light, notice the path, listen to your introducer, relax your body a little bit and check the mic to make sure it's on. When you step onto that stage, you are ready to deliver your speech with power and to truly be of value to that group.

LESSON 4

FIRST THINGS FIRST
- CONNECT!

What is the first thing you're going to do in a speech? **Connect** with *your* audience!. When you get onto that platform, look them in the eye and say something that causes them to feel a connection with you. Sometimes, I'll walk onto a stage for a Sales Training class and say, '**How many of you** have ever gone out to buy something, found what you wanted at a decent price but then you refused to buy it because you just didn't like the way the person was selling it? **How many**?' Hands go up all over the room.

I've already set the context for my speech. I've shown that it's a sales training presentation. I've talked about a topic that I could take in the direction of customer service. I've shown the audience, by raising my own hand, that I expect them to raise their hand. I've involved the audience with an open-ended question.

Other times, I'll step up on the stage and say, '*Good morning, (and as I look toward my introducer) thank you very much.*' I'll acknowledge my introducer and then I'll say something related to the context of the current scenario. One time, I was speaking to a large group in the round. I had a group seated behind me, as well as beside me and in front of me. It was a formal meeting, so I said 'Thank you,

Madam Chairman. Good morning, distinguished guests. Good morning, ladies and gentlemen.' Then, I went on with my speech. Sometimes, it is necessary to do those protocols. Every time, the first thing you want to do is connect with your audience. Clarify that connection!

33

Set the Context

Then, set the context. What are you going to talk about? Why? What's the purpose of this speech today? With my illustration a minute ago about the sales question, I set the context for that particular speech. Make contact, set the context, and stop any other thoughts that are going on in your mind and any other thoughts that may be going on in their minds about something other than what you're there to speak about.

What do you want to do first? Connect with the people! (**Make the connection!**)

LESSON 5

HOW TO STRUCTURE
A SPEECH

Many years ago, before I was working as a full-time, professional speaker, I was selling training materials. This was back in my home state of Arkansas. I got a call, one Sunday, from a friend who was a preacher. He had a little community church out in the country, outside of Little Rock, and his name was Bill Patrick. He said 'Jim, you're preaching Sunday.' I said, 'Yeah, right. Bill, I'm not a preacher and I'm not preaching Sunday.' He said, 'No, you're preaching Sunday. I need you.' I asked, 'What do you mean?' He said, 'Well, I've got an engagement in Boston, I've got to fly out of town. I'm not going to be here Sunday. I know you; I trust you; you've met some of the people in my church, I want you to deliver the sermon on Sunday.' I said 'Gosh, what am I going to do? I don't know how.' He told me, 'Jim, just pray about it and think about it, you'll do fine.'

3 Points, 3 Stories, Close

I thought that was a dangerously loose approach to it. I needed a little more structure to feel comfortable, but I said, 'Okay, I'll do that.' I gave it some serious thought. I did pray about it and I thought, if I'm going to deliver a sermon, what am I going to talk about? What would the people find valuable? I decided that I would talk about spiritual growth, how to grow in your own belief system and your own practicing of your beliefs. That became my subject focus and then I did something that a friend had suggested. He said, 'Come up with three points, develop three stories to go with the points, and then conclude.'

I remember this vividly because I was so worried going into it, it made a clear imprint in my **mind** and *emotions.* First, know what you believe. Figure out what it is that you actually believe. Explore the works of the Bible or whatever scriptures you're studying. Explore the works of your beliefs and see what you really believe. Know what you believe; I told a little story connected to that belief.

Second, study, test and explore what you believe. Meaning, take what you believe and put it to work. Put it out in the sunlight and get some exposure to other points of view and potential criticism and see if it stands up to the criticism. If it doesn't, maybe you don't really believe it. Maybe you've just been reciting someone else's beliefs and you hadn't figured out your own beliefs yet. Second, explore, test, and study your beliefs. Third, live your beliefs. If you believe it, it will show up in your actions. If it's really a part of you, it will be present in your life. I talked about living your beliefs and I gave a story for each of those three points and then I concluded.

That speech probably had more impact than maybe 50 other speeches I've given in my life, because it was tightly focused, it was clearly structured so people could understand it and relate to it. It was illustrated with a story for each of the three points and then I concluded and called for action - I suggested to each and every one in the congregation they implement these ideas.

The Cathcart Method™ of being natural, focused and intentional, can be applied with any genre from business to political or even a day at school with one of your kids. Choose a topic, your three points, your stories, a very short example, conclude and ask the people to do something with what they just learned.

I hear and I forget.
I see and I remember. I do and I understand.

LESSON 6

ON-SITE PREPARATION TIPS

From more than 40 years now, I've been working as a professional speaker. One of the primary skill sets for professional speakers is on-site preparation. When you're already at the meeting, what can you do to prepare? You've already done your speech preparation. You studied the organization. You've prepared your notes for the speech. You know what you're going to talk about, things like that. But, what about on-site? Well, on-site, the first thing is to increase your awareness. Go check out the meeting room. Find out how the hotel or the property is structured.

Know your Surroundings!

Look around and identify the locations of every single Fire Exit. If you're standing up there speaking and a fire breaks out or some kind of emergency happens, you will be the person in charge. You've got the microphone! You're the one who's going to have to tell people which direction to go.

Prepare your awareness about the client too. What's going on with the client? Where do you fit in the meeting? Take a look at the materials that have the agenda for the meeting. Talk to some of the other people there, get a sense of what's going on and what the variables are. Prepare your awareness.

Prepare Your Voice, Mind and Mood

Next, before you speak, make sure you get some private time to prepare your voice. Do some exercises to loosen up your voice. Breathe deeply, do some physical exercise that will get the blood flowing in your body. Make sure you're fully alert and ready to deliver your message well. Next, prepare your mind, get the right thinking for this. Review your notes. Find out about the organization. Go back through some of the research you've done for that speech. It's what I call 'putting it on your desktop.' It's okay to have a whole lot of files in your computer but if you don't get them on your desktop then you don't have access to it right now. The same thing is true for a speech. Get it out of the files, open the folders, and in front of your mind. You say, 'I already know this stuff.' Yeah, but do you know it well enough you could just rattle it off like that? Put it in front of your mind. It's not what you know that counts; it is what you can recall at the instant you need it.

Next, prepare your mood. You need the right emotions to deliver the kind of presentation that you're there to deliver. Cultivate the feelings and think about the reason for your speech. So, be in the right mood for it. If you're not a good mood, if you're not in an appropriate mood, don't give the speech yet. Find a way to get yourself in the right mood and prepare your awareness of your client.

See what they're going through. Not just understanding the company, understand the industry, understand the audience, and understand what each person is going through right now. Are they juggling 15 other things and having trouble keeping up? Are they really on top of things and having a wonderful time? Are they worried about whether you can do your job well? Know about your client, understand them as fully as you can and prepare your tools.

Prepare the tools of your trade. Whether it's notes, whether it's your microphone, whether it's a place where you can stand the lighting you're going to use, know the tools. It's embarrassing to see some unprofessional speakers stand up in front of a group and start fidgeting with the microphone. *"Tap, tap, tap. Is this on? Can you hear me okay? Can you guys hear me?"* Or, just stand there in front of the group and work on their laptop during the speech as if the audience had disappeared. That's like a professional musician coming out for the opening of a concert and tuning the instrument instead of performing for the audience. Extremely unprofessional. So, prepare your tools. Be ready, when it's your moment, when the introduction has happened, to step up and deliver a message with power, with charisma and with impact on the people who are listening to you.

LESSON 7

WHEN DOES A SPEECH REALLY BEGIN?

The speech begins when you leave home.   Let me explain what I mean. Years ago, I was going to Santa Fe, New Mexico to participate in a program. When I got to the airport in San Diego where I was living at the time, I saw a man who was checking in at the same time I was, at the main desk. I nodded to him; he nodded back. I went ahead and checked it. I went to the gate; he was on the same flight. Got on a plane, he was two rows back behind me. Got to Phoenix, he changed to the same flight I changed to. We got to Albuquerque and got off the plane, he walked to the same spot on the curb that I walked to. Obviously, we had similar itineraries.

Finally, I turned, and I spoke to him. I said, 'Hi, I'm Jim Cathcart.' He said, 'I'm Jack Cima.' I said, 'Jack, where are you going?' He said, 'I'm going to a program in Pecos.' I said, 'So am I.'

We were going to exactly the same program! We both lived in San Diego yet didn't know each other. Knew a lot of other people in common. Now, imagine for a minute that I didn't know that, and I just went blissfully about my business thinking the speech doesn't begin until I get to the speaking venue, okay? Maybe I'm having a bad day that day and so I snap at people or I'm rude or I'm kind of sullen. What impression would I be giving to Jack, who is going to be in my audience the next day? The speech begins when you leave home.

One time I was standing in line at a McDonald's in Jonesboro, Arkansas on my way to a Jaycees meeting. I remember the guy behind me kept bumping into me and it was really annoying me. He bumped into me again and again and finally, I decided to say something. Just as I took a breath to firmly tell

39

this guy to stop bumping into me, the guy in line behind him said, '*You're Jim Cathcart, aren't you?*' I said yes. He said, '*I saw you speak in Pine Bluff the other day. Great job!*' Whew, I was about to embarrass myself in front of a previous audience member. When you're a speaker, you've got a much bigger audience than you know. Any time you're going to a meeting, make sure that when you are at the taxi stand, when you're in the airport shuttle, when you're in the hotel lobby, the hallways, that you are conscious of how you treat others and what kind of message that's conveying to people.

Don't Embarrass Yourself

One time, a keynote speaker and his wife were at the same meeting, which had not yet convened. After dinner, before the meeting, they decided to have some fun on the elevator, not considering THEIR surroundings. They had not met the people who had hired him to speak. They got on the crowded elevator acting as if they didn't know each other. He leaned over toward her and smelled her perfume. He said, '*Excuse me miss, but you look wonderful.*' She said, '*Thank you very much, you're kind of handsome yourself.*' He said, '*I'm not doing anything later this evening and I wonder if you'd come up to my room and share a glass of champagne with me?*' She said, '*I'll stay the night. What do you like for breakfast?*' The elevator stopped and they got off on their floor. They laughed all the way down the hallway because they had just pulled one over on the people in the elevator. Later that night, he stepped onto the stage to give a speech. In the front row, right directly in front of him, was the chief executive of the organization that had hired him to speak. It was the guy who was on the elevator behind them.

Oops! You're always on stage, you never know when this is going to come across to someone else.

LESSON 8

HOW TO CONNECT WITH YOUR AUDIENCE? LRAMA

I had a very good friend who passed away not too long ago, a terrific speaker. His name was Lee Shapiro, he was a judge. He called himself the hugging judge. He always encouraged people to hug each other. He said, you need a few hugs each day just to survive. He was a very happy guy, with a very, very positive message. One of the things that he told me that he did -that impressed me a lot- he said, 'in my speech notes, I always right in the upper right-hand corner, LMA.' I asked, what does that mean? He said, 'it means love my audience and it encourages me to cultivate a strong caring, a feeling toward my audience.' I thought that's a good idea so here's how I use it. I write LRAMA, which means like, respect and admire my audience. LRAMA: like, respect, and admire my audience.

When I'm sitting there in the meeting room prior to my speech, I look at them and I think positive thoughts about them. I think about what could I notice that would cause me to like them even more? I try to cultivate that attitude of I like you. Also, I look for something I respect about this group, something that I could comment on from the platform that would cause them to feel a little bit better, to feel honored that I brought it up. What do I admire about them? Maybe what I admire about them is that they stayed with it through a very tough time. Even if the company hasn't done particularly well and I'm speaking to that company's audience, at least I can admire the fact that they didn't get out of the business, or they didn't do unethical things in order to make things better. There's always something you can find to admire.

As you read through the materials, as you prepare for a speech, look for things to like, things to respect, and things to admire which you can even point out in your speech itself. Another time, I was in a seminar - this was a long time ago, late 1970s. I was in the seminar, and I think it was Dave Yoho who's one of the founding members of the National Speakers Association. He was speaking about speaking and he said enter, involve, contact. Enter the audience, in other words, what he wanted to do first thing in his speech was step into the group a little bit. Involve the group was number two, enter and involve. He would ask for a show of hands or an answer to a question or have them all stand or sit. Then, the third thing was contact. Make some contact with the audience whether that's intellectual contact, whether it's verbal contact, whether it's physical contact or shaking someone's hand or whatever. That was his formula.

Whatever you do, when you first get up on that platform, the things that you do in those first moments will set the context for what they expect and how they get involved in that particular speech. I remember one time Zig Ziglar stepped on the platform in Tulsa, Oklahoma, late 70s early 80s. He was there for a big sales rally. He walked out, stopped, planted his feet, looked at the audience and said 'there are five reasons and five reasons only why your customer will not buy from you tomorrow. No trust, no money, no hurry...' he went on with the five. I remember that clearly today and it's been 30 years since he delivered that speech. What you do in the first few moments leaves an impression on that audience, it matters.

One time I was in Anaheim. I was sitting in the back of the room, had one of my staff members with me. We were looking at the meeting and the meeting was not being particularly well-run, and it was poorly organized. The introductions were awkward, the transitions from speaker to speaker were slow, and there were times when there was nobody at all on the stage and everybody was sitting there wondering what was coming next. A lot of things were poorly done; the room wasn't laid out in a very effective manner. My staff member was sitting there and criticizing, *'Can you believe these people?*

Look at this.' I said, *'Excuse me, that may be true, but I can't afford to think about this audience the way you're talking about this audience. That may be true but if I cultivate that awareness, when I get on that stage it will come across as being better than them or it will come across as being arrogant or judgmental.*

I need to think about these people as individuals about what their job is and what my message has to do with how they can do better.' He said, 'You're absolutely right.' He zipped his lip and I sat there and gathered my thoughts, and the speech went fine.

It really does matter what you do in the first few minutes, and it matters how you begin those first few minutes in your own mind. So, give it some thought; enter, involve, contact. Like, respect, and admire your audience. Cultivate a positive attitude toward them. It will come back to you.

HOW TO END YOUR SPEECH

How do you end a speech? Well, end it completely. There are a lot of people who just wander into the end of their speech, you don't know whether they're done and then finally they just stop talking. Other people will wait until they can build up to some huge crescendo. I think the main thing to end the speech is just summarize what you said to them. Go back over some your key points, emphasize the purpose, restate the purpose for the speech in the first place. For example, you might say *'if we raise our level of customer service and satisfaction, then we will get a higher ranking which will qualify us for a higher level of rewards from the organization itself. So, let's focus on improving that customer service index and let's remember that the three keys are going to be, (describe 1, 2, and 3). Thank you very much.'* You step off the stage. Restate the purpose of your speech, review the main points, tell the people what to do with it now, and then call for action. Make it clear that your speech is over.

LESSON 10

WHEN TO END YOUR SPEECH

Have you ever been in the audience listening to a speaker who didn't know when to quit or maybe didn't know how to quit? Sometimes they just keep looking for the ending like somehow it's going to magically appear in their mind or in their voice and then they'll end. As to knowing when to quit, let me just make it simple for you. You should quit speaking just before they quit listening. Is that fair? We need to make sure that as long as we have something interesting and valuable to say and as long as it is appropriate for us to be on that stage in front of that group at that time, we ought to still be speaking.

But, when your time's up, stop the speech.

We need to stay conscious of the time and it's okay to look at your watch. It's not unprofessional to glance at your watch but if you do it too often it's going to distract the audience. Most of the time, if you look at your watch, they'll look at their watch shortly thereafter. But, if you can find a way to just discreetly look at your watch once or twice during the speech or if you have your watch sitting on the lectern while you're speaking, you can glance at it without any distractions but stay conscious of the time and respect the agenda. There are many subtle ways to use your computer, smartphone or other tools to stay on time.

For other people's sake, if there's another speaker or another event after you, don't run overtime. You might say, 'Now, wait a minute. *They told me I was going to get an hour and I got introduced late. I'm going to take my whole hour.*' But I say, don't take your whole hour, be a professional. Speak within the timeframe that was allotted for your presentation and if you got a late start, don't run overtime. At the end of your speech put them back on their agenda, put their meeting back on time. They'll respect and admire you for doing it. Just cut out a few things from the speech that might not be essential to the message or the impact of the message.

I tell you; a lot of speakers don't know how to do that. They think, *well, all of this material is great and if I leave this out, gosh, they're going to notice.* No, they're not. They don't know what your outline is, they don't know what you're about to cover. So, if you leave a portion of it out, it's not going to occur to them at all, unless what you left out changed the logic of what you were presenting. If you run out of material, if you've already covered the material you have, stop speaking.

Let me give you an example. I was in Iowa one time, and I was scheduled to speak to a group of people who were highly technical people. They were not accustomed to interacting with their presenters. This was fairly early in my speaking career; it was the first few years of it. I had a three-hour time frame, and I prepared my material. The way I prepare my material, I assume that I'm going to get at least 20% of the time in interaction with the audience and the 80% of the time will be made presenting. Depending on the type of audience, I might even increase the percentage that calls for or allows for customer involvement. Well, in this particular speech, the audience involvement or customer involvement was zero. I couldn't - for the life of me - get them to respond to anything. They seem to be interested, they wrote some things down, but they weren't interacting with me at all.

As I went on speaking, I kept covering more and more material earlier than I expected to and I was done with the speech, and I had a half hour of time left. A half hour. As I was approaching that half hour, I thought about what I was going to do. Finally, it occurred to me, the worst thing I could do is try to stretch and fill the time. So, when I got to the end of my material, I summarized what I was talking about, I restated the main point that was the purpose of the presentation, I told them how to use the ideas, and I concluded a half hour early. The client did not criticize it. He was surprised that I ended a half hour early, but I told him that it was lack of responsiveness on part of the audience. Then we talked to some of the audience members, they were getting the value they wanted from it, we had just chosen the wrong time frame for the material I was presenting. Whew, dodged that bullet, huh?

When you're done, they're done. Don't stretch to fill it. If they get done listening before you get done speaking, find a way to wrap it up and stop the presentation. The worst thing you can do is drag it on if they're through listening. One of the quickest ways to make sure they're still listening is let them contribute. Ask them for examples or ideas. Ask them about one of your main points, how they would apply that point and involve the audience. If they don't participate, they don't feel connected to you, so they don't feel nearly as much like they've invested emotionally in the presentation. So, use stories because stories capture people's imagination. Use actions having people move or raise their hands or write something down or actions involved with them physically. Use questions. When you ask the question *'how many of you...'* then raise your own hand indicating you expect them to raise their hands. Use visuals because that involves people on a different level. And, use your own movement to have some meaning that relates to your presentation. All of these will help you stay connected with a group so that you keep speaking while they keep listening. When they're done listening, you're already done speaking.

LESSON 11

HOW TO DRESS FOR EACH SPEECH

Dress for Success

How should you dress for a speech? The answer is appropriately. Dress in a way that's appropriate for the setting and your role within it. Don't just dress for the way the audience is going to be dressed, dress for the role that you're playing at that meeting. If you're the master of ceremonies then dress for the role of master of ceremonies. Don't necessarily dress the same as you would if you were delivering a keynote address or if you were a member of the audience. Some people say well, you dress like they dress. I disagree.

Dress just a step more formal or more professionally than the audience is dressed because after all, you're presenting ideas. You're there to fill a role that is a role of teaching, educating, leading, guiding, influencing people. In order to do that, you need to have the look that goes along with the message so dress appropriately to the group. You might ask, let's say you're an accountant, how would this group expect an expert accountant, an accountant who could teach them something, to dress? Dress to go with the role that you're playing at the meeting. You can always go down a step, it's harder to go up a step.

For example, I could come into a meeting dressed in a suit. I can easily take off the jacket and create a more relaxed look. I could go a step further and take off the tie, roll up my sleeves. There are a lot of things that I could do to be more relaxed. But, it would be really hard to come in there with my sleeves rolled up, no tie on, and in front of the group put on a tie and then put on a jacket and go in the opposite direction. Obviously there are different approaches between men and women. When you're dressing for a presentation, remember that your attire, your appearance, your grooming is part of your message.

They're going to be listening to that while they're listening to what you have to say.

HOW TO RECOVER FROM A BAD INTRODUCTION

Did you ever get a bad introduction? Did you ever have someone get your name wrong or even deliver the wrong bio for somebody else instead of for you? I've had that happen. Of course, I've been doing this for over 40 years, so I've had just about all the bad introductions happen. I've had a person say '*Okay, here he is, Jim Catchright*'. (Cathcart's the name, not Catchright, Cartwright, Cartwell.) I have seen them come up with all kinds of variations on it. Sometimes a person just gets flustered and they're nervous and they get the whole thing wrong.

One day I was in Nebraska and was scheduled to give a speech and I looked at the program for the convention. There's a picture of me and it was a picture from 10 years ago, so it looked like a picture of my son instead of a picture from me, and a bio from another guy. The bio wasn't even me! It was another guy who had the same last name, but it was a totally different individual, from a totally different business. So, when I stood up to speak, I said, '*Would everyone please get out your program? Would you turn over to the page that has a picture of a guy that looks like I used to?*' And they all kind of chuckled. I said, '*That's a picture of me from 10 years ago. I owe you an apology. We sent, evidently, from my office the wrong photo and somewhere in the mix, another person's bio got mixed in there.*

That bio right there, if you would, just make a big X through that, that's not me. Let me tell you who I am and why I'm here to talk to you today.' I had some fun with the group, and I made sure not to embarrass the meeting planner. I took the blame. I put it on my organization, not on them. That would've been really awkward had I blamed their own people for messing up. Not a good idea and certainly not a good way to start. So, we had a little fun with it and I got a chance to tell them why I should be speaking to them at this time on the subject.

Another thing that happens is sometimes you'll get an introducer who will do the wrong name or the wrong facts about you and you choose not to respond to it because sometimes it's not worth the effort. Sometimes it's not a big enough error that it is worth correcting. Just jump into your message and deliver the speech you came to deliver.

The Gusher

One time a speaker was introduced by a person who really admired him. This person got up there and just gushed, '*Oh, this is the most wonderful person! Oh, leading authority! Primary thinker, one of the great people of our generation. Blah, blah, blah, gush, gush, gush*.' By the time the speaker got up there, you expected it to be the second coming of Christ or something. This was going to be a big deal. But, he was an ordinary man. What he did, I thought was brilliant. He stepped to the microphone. He said, '*Thank you very much. Let's get right to business*.' He looked at the group in a serious manner, jumped right into his material, didn't even acknowledge the size and an intensity of that introduction.

He just did a polite acknowledgment and went right into his speech. It was very good. Choose what you're going to do in a case like that. You don't have to respond directly to it or you can respond specifically if you want to. If they give too little information, maybe you want to add to it. You might want to say, 'You might be asking yourself, how come I'm speaking to you on this subject? What do I know about this? Let me tell you what I've experienced and who I have been exposed to that might give you a little insight into why I'm talking on this subject today. Then, you give them a little of your own bio. If the other person has given you a *really* bad introduction, meaning if they've ruined the mood toward your presentation, then you've got some repair work to do.

Terrible Intro

One time, I went into a medical meeting room. It was one of these tiered seating arrangements where you walk down into the pit. This was at a college, a medical University. The doctor who was speaking before me, this was a practice management seminar that was being done for a bunch of newly graduated doctors or actually about to graduate doctors. This doctor had made a ruling they didn't get the chance after completing their curriculum to go home and spend a couple weeks with their family which the previous classes had always done. They had to stay at the school and go through a couple weeks of practice management training in addition to their medical training before graduation. They all resented being there. This was the guy; my introducer was the guy who made that decision, and they hated him. They'd love to have seen him just stuck with a spear and set on fire in front of the room. It was hideous the feelings between these people and he's my introducer, for heaven's sake!

He gets up on stage and he looks at them and he says, '*You're behaving like children. You might as well snap out of it and just sit up straight and pay attention. You've got to be here anyway. You don't have any choice, so get over it. Now, we brought in a motivational speaker, his name's Jim Cathcart. Maybe he can do something with you*' and he left the room. I almost died; I saw my whole life pass in front of my face. I mean I was terrified, what a horrible introduction! I had three days with these people, an hour and a half each morning for three consecutive mornings. I was in a panic. So, I stumbled up there and I said some lame thing about I'm not here to motivate you, motivation comes from within. I stumbled through it. I did okay. The second day I came back and did a little better and the third day a little bit better, but it never did quite click.

Now, this was back in the 1980s. I remember reading the evaluations. Boy, I'll tell you if you're in a situation where you know you blew it, don't read the evaluations. All that is going to do is just deepen your depression. I read the evaluations, I remember they were all sarcastic type comments about the meeting and one of them said, '*Cathcart seems like a nice enough guy, why are you doing this to him?*' When you get a terrible introduction just remember it's not about you. It's about them, it's about what's going on the room. If I were doing that again today, now, I have enough separation from it emotionally, I could think about it and do something wiser.

Learn from a Failure

Today, what I would've said is, '*How many of you actually believe you need motivating?*' I would've looked out, they probably wouldn't have responded at all. I'd say, '*That's what I expected. I'm not here to motivate you today. I'm here because you guys are here and there's a curriculum and we can approach this in one of two ways. We can all sit here and resent it, we can continue to cultivate any anger we have about this, or we can see if we can get some value out of it. So, I'll tell you what. I'll do my job. If you feel like joining in, by all means, do. I'm going to present several ideas and I'd love to have your questions. I'd love to be able to help make this meaningful to you. So, let's see what we got.*' Then, I would've gone on with presentation with no demands on them and probably would've found that several of them would've gotten involved, ultimately. So, when you get a bad introduction, don't let it blow your whole presentation. Don't take it personally, see it as situational and see that it's a statement about the other people, about their relationships, about any number of other things. But, do your job.

Do what you're there to do. If you have to just do the presentation and get it over with without any audience support then do it. If you can take them a different direction, win their support, do that as well.

LESSON 13

HOW TO MANAGE YOUR OWN FIRST IMPRESSION

I think we can manage our own first impressions. If we're conscious of how we come across to other people, especially at a meeting where we're going to be the speaker. It's kind of likely that your name or your picture is going to be in the program for that meeting. People are going to be watching for someone who either looks like you or has a name tag with your name on it or something like that. What you do will be noticed more than what other people might do.

Be Approachable

Something that we want to be sure and do as speakers, is to appear to be approachable. Look like a real person not like a suit. Be, not an outsider to the group but a person who is a friend of the group who has come there to share some ideas with them. Even if you're a celebrity, if you're not a very high lofty position - from their point of view - the more approachable, the more natural, the more friend-like you can appear, the more likely you are to be well received by that audience. The last thing in the world they want is for somebody to just stand there and look important or to bless them with pearls of wisdom from above. They want someone to look them in the eye and relate to them directly. By the way, pay attention to this in the hallways, in the restaurant, out at the taxi stand, when you're in the shuttle to and from the airport. Wherever it happens to be, you're going to run into other people and those people may end up in your meeting. So, manage your first impression and know that you're building a first impression from the moment you get ready to go to that speech.

LESSON 14

HOW TO CHANGE THE MINDSET OF YOUR AUDIENCE

I was in Atlanta; I was speaking to 3000 people. The speaker before me got up and he said, '*Alright folks, it's a dog-eat-dog world out there so you've got to bite first, you got to bite hard and never quit biting.*' That was his sales message. He was telling them to go out there as a combatant and fight the world.

Then, I was introduced to speak on the subject of **Relationship Selling**! Seemed like a complete contradiction of what he was just talking about. On the fly, I had to figure out, how to make the bridge from this aggressive, confrontational attitude to the one I was about to present. Imagine going from confrontational to how to connect with people in such a way that they want to give you all their business. I thought about it, realizing the dilemma, I made a few notes to myself.

When I got up to speak I said, "*You know folks, sometimes it is a dog-eat-dog world and maybe you have to bite first, bite hard and keep on biting but if your customer ever gets the sense that you're about to bite, you'll lose all their business. Would you agree?*" They said, "Yeah!" I said, "*So let's talk about how you practice relationship selling in a way that you can still win the business and still dominate the marketplace.*" And, I went on and I focused on my message, and it seemed to go well. What you have to do is just show courtesy to the people who came before you and be clear on what your own message is. Courtesy and clarity.

Build a bridge for them from that previous attitude to your own or you may choose, in some cases, not to even acknowledge the previous message and just start fresh with your own. Let them do the transition. Know that it is needed. Just recognize that something's going on there and there is a disconnect between what they just heard what you're about to say and then make a judgment call as to whether you're going to address it or whether you're going to let them just handle it on their own.

LESSON 15

SELL YOUR AUDIENCE ON THE VALUE OF THIS MEETING

I did something the other day that got such a great response from my client I thought I'd share it with you. I was talking to the group about the value of learning. I said, "A lot of people talk about these meetings and say I came home and thought about the meeting, and you know where the greatest value was? In the hallways. Talking with the people over dinner. Talking with them in the hallways between the meetings. We could've done without the meetings entirely, just get together and talk with each other.'"

Well, I can understand how people would come to that conclusion but that's not the reality. The reason the time in the hallways and the time over dinner and the time on the golf course is so valuable is because all of you have been together in the same meeting, listening to the same messages. The presentations from the platform, the events where new products are introduced and the other things that happen at the meeting, all of them fit into the mix.

The blend of all those things lead to some really valuable discussions in the hallways, over dinner, and on the golf course. I pointed out to the group the value of all of that and how much work had been put into this meeting on the part of meeting planner. The meeting planner felt like a hero, the audience acknowledged that there was value in all of that, and I scored some serious points with my client. Take time to remind people of the value they are receiving and how.

LESSON 16

PODIUM OR NO PODIUM? STAND ON NOT BEHIND

Should you have a podium or not? Well, first off, let's get clear on what a podium is. Podium comes from the word *pod*, indicating feet. In other words, a podium is something you stand on, it's not something you stand behind. That's a lectern or rostrum or a speaker stand. In today's society, podium has come to be used as the popular word for rostrum or lectern or speaker stand. So, if you have an actual podium, what is a podium? It's a small platform for one person. Just recognize that if you're requesting a podium, they might give you a little platform instead of a speaker stand. Be clear on what you're asking for. I usually try to use the word *lectern* instead of *podium*. If they come back and say, oh, you want a podium? Then, I say fine and I just go with it because it's become the popular interpretation of that word. But, a podium - in the lectern sense of podium - often becomes a barrier between you and the audience.

Recognize that it's going to do something to the dynamics between you and the people you're speaking to. It's okay to have it there but make sure it's low enough that they can see plenty of your upper body and your face. Make sure the lighting is good enough that they can see your facial expressions and you can make eye contact with them. If it's a large group, make sure that there's a camera on you and the big screen is showing the projection of you so that you can get a sense of closeness with the audience through the size of that image. Otherwise, it's best to step out from behind that lectern and to address the audience in more of a natural way.

What's the purpose of your presentation? Is it to be formal and do something ceremonial? Or, is it to lead them through an intellectual exercise?

Is it to connect with them personally and to emotionally impact their feelings about something? Whether you use the lectern or not will depend on the purpose.

Years ago, I was in Concord, New Hampshire to give a speech to the Concord Prison Jaycees (Junior Chamber of Commerce). In the prison, I was led into a big auditorium/gymnasium combination. They brought in a bunch of park benches and put them all around the room and the inmates sat on those park benches.

I was up on the stage which was four feet high from the floor. They not only had a head table, they had a lectern behind the head table. Anyone who was speaking, felt like they were two blocks away from the audience. Not only were they way above them but they were back away from them. I realized when the first few people were speaking at that meeting that I was going to make no contact with that audience at all if I stayed up there in that remote location.

Remove Any Barriers

So, as soon as I was introduced, I acknowledged the introduction and then I stepped off the stage and down onto the gymnasium floor where the people were seated. I said, 'Let me come down here so we can talk.' And, when I did, I noticed they sat up a little straighter, they paid more attention, and the presentation went well. Now, that's a very strange environment but those same dynamics are present in a lot of business environments. Just do whatever you can to remove the barriers between you and your audience. Make the connection in the best way you can.

LESSON 17

HEAD TABLES ARE DEAD!

Head tables are dead! That's right, head tables. They are a product of a bygone era. It's time we outgrew them. The purpose of head tables comes from a time when it was important to separate the leaders from the followers, the superiors from the subordinates, the royalty from the common people. If you trace the history of head tables, it goes back to the days when royalty would sit at a raised table, and they would dine while the common folk would sit down below and observe the royalty dining. In other words, it was clearly a message to the rest of the group that these people were special, they were important. As a matter of fact, they were more important and that's why they got to sit at the head table.

You might say there's still a place for that. Well, yes, in a way, but the head tables are not the way to do it. We've outgrown that era. We have media and technology now. We are accustomed to going to meetings now. We are now a society that is much more welcoming of each other, much more respectful of each other, regardless of rank and privilege. So, head tables don't do the job that they used to do.

There's still a way you can do this. You say, '*Well, I want to have special reserved seating for the dignitaries, the VIPs, the visiting celebrities, the company executives and so forth.*' Fine, have reserved seating up front but for the purposes of the meeting, let the speaker speak, let the events and the presentations get the full attention of the audience. At the same time, acknowledge your leaders of the organization by having reserved seating on the main floor level, perhaps red tablecloths - may be in the front rows - but on the main floor with the rest of the folks. Next, have a stage that is slightly raised (appropriate to the size of the room), have a speaker-stand if you want to, have a chair if it's appropriate.

Stage is for Speeches

Make sure there is plenty of light on the speaker, Make sure everyone in the room can see and hear them and not be distracted by watching someone else making notes, talking to the person next to them, picking fruit from their teeth or still eating a meal that was served at the event. Get those things out of the line of sight. Have the reserved tables for the VIPs, if you choose to, but let the stage be a place for the speeches.

LESSON 18

SPEAKING IN THE ROUND

On my 40th birthday, which was a while ago, my wife Paula presented me with tickets to a concert. The concert was a Neil Diamond concert, it was in San Diego, California. We went into this enormous sports arena, and we found that the seats we had, which were bought over the telephone, were the worst possible seats in the house. I mean you could've checked it out and spent hours trying to determine, you couldn't find worse seats than we had in that venue. We were behind the stage, way at the top of the seating area leaning back against the rafters. We were as far from the stage as you could get in the area behind the stage. Well, bless Neil Diamond's heart, that night he cared about the audience enough that every so often he would come around behind the stage and present to the people in the back for a minute or two. Then, go back to the front of the stage.

Now, today, we would have big screens and they'd be for all the people in the room so you could see him fully whether you were behind the stage or in front, but they didn't have it back then. When you are put in a position where you have to speak in the round, of course, you're not going to have all the bells and whistles in most cases like a professional performer would.

The Cathcart Method™ Turn your Head First

If you have to speak with people on all sides of you, there are some techniques that can make that a little easier. For one thing, don't just spin. Don't get up there and talk around and around like a whirling dervish. You're going to drive people nuts, make them dizzy, and you're also going to throw yourself off balance. Instead, speak to each part of the audience for a minute and then speak to another part of the audience. Don't just go in a 1-2-3-4, like a clock. Speak to this group over here, then turn and acknowledge those folks over there and speak to them. Turn your head first and then your body.

Sometimes you can talk to this group over here and look back and talk to that group and say something to them and then come back to this group for a minute.

Just be purposeful about it and make sure that there's not a person in the audience you didn't look at once, at least. Sometimes when you're sitting in the audience you can't tell for sure where a person is looking. Now, maybe the person on the platform is looking at someone three rows behind you but because of the angle from the platform to the audience you feel like they're looking you square in the eyes. Did you ever get that feeling? Sometimes, when you're just looking in that direction, you have maybe as many as 30 to 50 people who think they have direct one-to-one eye contact communication with you. Learn to cultivate that technique and you'll be far more effective in speaking.

CARDS, NOTES, HANDOUTS OR NONE?

Cards, notes, handouts or none? You make the call. What do you think? Should you use your notes, should you have them in your hand? Now, I've seen speakers that do a very good job, stand in front of a group, and hold their notes in their hand and refer to them from time to time. Typically, when they do that, the audience has the same outline in front of them. If you and the audience are going through an outline, a handout together, that can be very effective. If they don't have a copy of it, it might seem a little distracting. I think it's completely okay to stand on a platform, deliver a speech and occasionally pick up the notes, put on the reading glasses if you need to, read something from the notes to them, and then go on with your speech, or to just have your notes handy, glance at them and make another point.

You can even refer to your notes. You can say, 'there was one other thing I want to be sure and say, oh, here it is.' and then share that idea with them. People don't mind that.

Note Cards Can be Limiting

Some people use the little 3 x 5 cards. Typically, those are not the professional speakers - not that it's unprofessional to do that. It's just that professional speakers seem to be less likely to use the little note cards. I've used those in the past, in the long distant past, and I just find that they're very limiting because you have to shuffle them and it's just a different technique.

The Cathcart Method™; Write an outline of your speech on one sheet of paper, one side. If you are using PowerPoint slides, take each slide and write the name of the slide or the identifier that tells what's on that slide in the left-hand margin. Then, next to it, make a note of the story you want to tell or a point you want to drive home.

I was in a seminar one time and the speaker had arrived early to set up his huge cue cards all along the front of the front table where the audience couldn't see them, but he could see them clearly. While he's standing there speaking, he's looking down at cue cards that he actually wrote for himself. He had some more sitting on the table next to where he was standing. That's fine if it works for you and it doesn't distract the audience. Go for it. Now, PowerPoint® has technology that allows you to see your notes at the same time the audience is seeing the slide.

There are a lot of ways you can go about this. But, the main thing I want to tell you is just don't get hung up on it. It's no big deal unless you make a big deal of it. Do what works and do what has the right effect on the people that you're going to be speaking with. One of my friends will plant certain responses with audience members. During his speech, when he comes to that particular part, he'll call out to that audience member and ask them for what the word was that he had given them. They'll give him a word and then he'll play off of that word and go into his next part of the speech and he'll go to another one over here and then one over there and then one back over here. You could do this with a grab bag drawing too. It gives him a way to involve the audience, in a very superficial way, but it draws them in and it makes them feel like they're part of what's going on. A lot of times I'll say, "I want to read something to you." I'll pick up my reading glasses and literally read to the audience from a text.

Then, I'll set it down and go on with my speech. It seems to work very well and a lot of times when you do that - even your notes become a prop and it works fine for the audience. Just make sure that you're comfortable with what you do and what you do is not done as if it was a secret only known to you. They know you've got notes and it's perfectly okay to use them.

SECTION 2

LESSON 20

HOW LONG SHOULD A STORY BE?

How long should a story be? As a general rule, maybe 3 to 5 minutes depending on the situation but sometimes it can be much longer than that. As a matter of fact, some entire speeches are stories. One story, the entire speech. I heard a speech recently where a man was telling of climbing Mount Everest and his entire speech was the story of the climb. There are also the stories that you use, the vignettes, little mini speeches that contain a story or an example. Those can be as long as you need them to be but you need to understand that every 3 to 5 minutes you're talking about a different speech almost.

I have a story that I call "The Grandma" story. I talk about going into a McDonald's one morning and getting some especially good service from a woman whose nickname was grandma. It takes about nine minutes to tell this story fully. Now, that's kind of long for a story, so what I do is I tell a portion of it. With some audiences I just stop after the first 3 to 5 minutes. With other audiences, I tell the entire story. The purpose of the short version and the long version are different.

It's all about the Purpose

In the longer version, I'm training. In the shorter version, I'm just illustrating a point, having some fun with the audience or driving home one idea. In the longer version, what I'll do is take the story apart. I'll say, 'Okay, why did she do that?' Here was the setting, here's the behavior, here's how the behavior worked. Why do you think she did that? You think she did that because she was paid to do it? Do you think she did what she did because there would've been punishment if she hadn't done it? Do you think she did because she was trained that way, it was in the training manual? Because it was expected? I have the audience with me dissecting this story and analyzing what would cause somebody to give the kind of good service she gave me. Then I have them ask, 'How can I use that in my own company?' I take those principles and apply it to their company.

The grandma story begins as a small little story about an experience in McDonald's then it becomes a customer service training capsule that I put inside another speech, a larger speech. It's okay to leave out parts of the story because if you leave out something the audience won't know it unless it disturbs the logic of the story.

One *Little* Thing Can Make a Huge Difference: Tim's Story

One story that I tell is a story about a man named Tim Seward. I met Tim when he was 19 years old, and I still know him today and he's in his 30s. Tim has come a long way over those years. When I tell the story this story, I talk about him when I first met him, I talk about how he started applying some ideas from the speech I'd given that day when he got home. Then, about the results he got from that and how he won a big award at the end of the year. Then, I tell yet another story about Tim, about what he's doing today and how he's become very wealthy and is semi-retired. Each of those is part of the same story but it's four parts in one story. I can tell just one part, just the first part or I can tell the first two or even the first three and not get to the other one, depending on what I need to accomplish in the speech. Let your stories expand and contract based on what you want to convey to your audience. Use it as a teaching tool and you'll find that you have more stories inside each story. Often, one little thing can make a huge difference in how well you get a point across.

LESSON 21

USING PROPS EFFECTIVELY

I wrote a book called The Acorn Principle. (Available on Amazon) Many times, I'll introduce it by holding up an acorn. I'll say, "If you start with an acorn, what will you ultimately have? Obviously, what you will ultimately have is an Oak tree." I talk about the Oak tree and the acorn and what it takes for an acorn to grow. I do a little vignette where I'm coaching an acorn to become a giant redwood, which by the way is impossible. I'll use that to emphasize that if a person doesn't recognize what kind of seed they have inside of them, they probably won't nurture it in the right way to be all that they're capable of being. Just a little simple prop that I can pack easily, and it reinforces the whole point of my book, **The Acorn Principle**: *Nurture Your Nature.*

Continuing Value of an Existing Customer

Another story that I tell is about the time I went into an automobile tire store to get my car repaired. I hold up a prop. What this prop is, is a list of repairs that I wanted done on the car back in 1986 and I've attached the actual receipts from the repair work that was done. I hold it up and talk about the car and the list and I tell the story about going into the dealership. Then, I say, 'What started out as a purchase of new tires ended up visit after visit after visit being a complete renovation of the automobile.' I just flip the pages and I just keep them coming and the people can see that these are real receipts. That these actually are the service records if they wanted to check. Then, I total it. On the back I have the actual total of all the repairs which was $9,620.72. Through the use of the simple prop, I really drive home the point about the continuing value of a customer that's built into that story that I tell about the repairs.

I talk about the value a customer holds to a dealership. Because when I came in there, I came in there to buy tires but when I ultimately sold the car, I had had $9600 worth of service done to it. Simple, one little prop can make your point very effectively.

Did We Care?

Here's one, most of the hotels we go in to have customer satisfaction surveys. They'll have a little form for you to fill out and send in. One that really impressed me was this one - not from a hotel but from Swiss Air. It has a woman's picture on the front and it's a feedback form like most of the others with the little questions. But, on the front of this card it says *Did We Care?* Wow, what a point. Did we care?

That's really what the customer wants to know. I used that to make my point about all these tools that we do for customer satisfaction or design really to convey to the customer that we really do care.

Here's a little thing I found in a hotel room one time. To our guests, in ancient times there was a prayer for the stranger within our gates. We'd like to share our version of that with you today.

> *May this room and hotel be your second home.*
> *May those you love be near you in thoughts and dreams.*
> *May the business that brought you this way prosper.*
> *When you leave, may your journey be safe and so forth.*

Good illustration of good customer service. Another thing I do, sometimes, is I'll talk about how you manage your people and how they feel about that. I read this from a newspaper, USA Today. It is a full-page ad that was purchased by the 16,000 (at that time) employees of Southwest Airlines to say Happy Boss' Day to Herb Kelleher, Chairman and President, the CEO of Southwest at that time. Key point driven home with a simple tool.

There's a seminar I do where I talk about how your attitude toward your customer shows up in simple things day-to-day. At a bank that I used to do business with, the receipt said *San Diego Trust and Savings Bank, where money matters but people count.* Then, it had a big bold statement of what your receipt was for. It says, *this is your receipt, please retain it to verify the transaction.* That's it. Then, they sold to First Interstate Bank. Here's First Interstate Bank's receipt. Same type of receipt, listen to what it says on this one. First off, notice that the big transaction amount on the San Diego Trust, which is easy to see, is now a tiny little imprint on the First Interstate. It says, *all credits for items are provisional until collected. All deposits involving checks are subject to final verification and adjustment. The bank may place a hold on all collected funds on any items you deposit, which could delay your ability to withdraw the funds. Retain receipt until verified.*

What feeling do you get from that one? The first one is friendly, open, it's simple. Tells you how much it's for. The second one tells you this is a legal transaction you'd better be careful. The way you think about your customers shows up in the things you do day-to-day. It's important to recognize that those messages are there. Here's another one, a correspondence between me and an airline or a couple of airlines. I use that to illustrate a specific scenario, story that I had when I was dealing with a particular organization. So, you can use props in any number of ways.

- You can use simple clips out of a newspaper
- A correspondence
- You can use ads; you can use anything that seems to make your point

The key, though, is to keep them out of sight until it's time for them to be used. When you are ready to expose the prop, for example, my acorn. Make sure you hold it up to the light, in clear sight so that your audience can see it clearly. Honor your prop. Treat it with respect. When I'm talking with the acorn in my hand or about the acorn, I hold it gently. I present it well; I don't just wave it around.

The Cathcart Method™ for Props
- Expose it when you want it exposed.
- We think in pictures - the prop adds value to your story
- Keep it hidden until then.
- Honor it

- Treat it with respect.
- When it's time to be done with it put it away.

Props can add so much to your presentation because they make a visual and thinking symbol that get imprinted in the mind of the listener.

LESSON 22

WRITE YOUR OWN
INTRODUCTION

Here's a tip to get your next speech off to a better start, write your own introduction. Not a resume, not a curriculum vitae (CV), not something that tells all the things that you've done but an introduction. An introduction that covers the basics like Dale Carnegie so often spoke about, why is *this* speaker speaking to *this* audience at *this* time on *this* subject? This speaker, this audience, this time, this subject. An introduction that explains those well serves the audience and the speaker very well. Whenever you're structuring an introduction add some fun to it. if it's appropriate to have fun in the introduction, make it easy for the other person to use and, for heaven sakes, coach your introducer so that your introducer is serving your purposes and building credibility for you or overcoming a miscommunication or something like that.

Here's the introduction that I typically use when I go out to speak professionally. I've written this exactly as I would like for them to use it. I even say on the introduction - you notice it's a fairly short introduction – Note to introducer: Please read this introduction exactly as written. It relates directly to some of the points that Jim will cover.

It says:

"Our speaker today is the founder and chief executive of Cathcart Institute. A team of business advisors who work with owners, leaders, and executives in the areas of executive development, professional speaking, and sales improvement. He is the author of 25 books, including two bestsellers, Relationship Selling, and The Acorn Principle. In the year 2000, the eBook edition of The Acorn Principle was the number two national bestseller out of 2000 eBook titles. Stephen King was number one."

Now, in that little introduction paragraph, what I've said is our speaker is the President of this organization and this organization works with the following types of people. So, I've done a little mini advertisement while building credibility. "He's the author of 25 books, 2 bestsellers" and I specify what those are. My eBook was one of 2000 titles chosen for the year 2000 and it came in number two nationally, as the bestseller, right behind Stephen King. The reason I said Stephen King's number one, if you tell anybody you're the number two or the number three in whatever, they're going to say I wonder who number one and two were? Might as well tell them.

Here's the second half of my introduction:

There's another side to our speaker that's even more interesting. He's also been a nightclub singer, a bartender, a bill collector, a psychological researcher, a motorcycle salesman, a banker, an insurance agent, a director of training, a meeting planner, association executive, and an Internet business owner. He may not be able to hold a job, but I hear he can really hold an audience.

Let's welcome Jim Cathcart.

Make Your Introduction Highlight Your Strengths with Humor

The reason I put *this guy can't hold a job* in there is to show my audience that I'm a regular guy, that I've done a lot of other things that are not necessarily the sort of things you'd expect a *suit* to do. And, at the end of it, when the person goes down that laundry list, I know the audience is thinking, *gosh, this guy can't hold a job*. Well, 40 years ago, it probably appeared that way. So, I just built in there, *he may not be able to hold a job, but I hear he can hold an audience. Let's welcome Jim Cathcart*. It starts on an upbeat, positive note. The introducer just had a good time and got a laugh at my expense. I made my credentials with the audience; things are going to go well.

LESSON 23

HOW TO SPEAK "AMONG" THE AUDIENCE

Do you ever need to speak out in the audience? If you do, handle it a little bit differently than you would when you're on the stage. For example, let's say you have light or sound problems, microphone goes out. What do you do? Do you stand there and wait for somebody to fix the problem? Do you try to fix it yourself and distract everybody? Or, do you ask someone for help and simply step into the audience and speak a little bit louder but speak from within the audience? This happened to me recently, I was in Colorado.

Think on Your Feet!

The meeting was held in a facility that was adjacent to my hotel and the hotel power went out. We were okay for a while but then something happened when they were fixing the power situation and the power went out in the conference center that was attached to the hotel. So, I'm standing there in the middle of a presentation using PowerPoint and all of a sudden my mic goes dead, the PowerPoint dies, the room goes dark. So, I had a decision to make. I said, "*Would someone please go back there and open up those window drapes so we can get some light into the room?*" And, a couple of people stepped up and took care of that. I came off of the platform and into the audience and I said, "*Obviously, we've lost power.*

Now, there are other folks addressing that problem right now. We can either take a break, which we just did a few minutes ago, or we can go on with the meeting. I say we go on with the meeting, what do you think?" They all said, "Yes." I just stepped into the middle of the group and continued my presentation.

A few minutes later, the slides came back up on the screen - the power was on - BUT whoever was dealing with the slides didn't know how to operate my computer, didn't know what files to look in and so forth. So, I ended up going without the slides for the balance of the presentation.

The Cathcart Method™ Learn the Lesson

Since that time, live and learn, I have put my PowerPoint slide presentations in a folder on the desktop of my computer called PowerPoint slide presentations. Each one of them, each file is titled with the name of that client and the date of that meeting. So, if it's Clarica life insurance, June 2, 2012, finding it is pretty easy, pretty much a no-brainer. If someone's looking around in there for the presentation, they can find it. I don't have to guide them through every step of the way.

Another thing, when you're in the audience, walk slowly and deliberately. Don't pace and don't race around the room. Just move from one point to another with a sense of purpose and try to involve everybody in the room. Stop when you want to make your point. Stand your ground: stand and deliver, as they say. It's much more powerful if you make a point with no movement and then illustrate your point with any amount of movement you want to use. Look at people all over the room. Sometimes, what's effective is if you go to one side of the room and you're a long way away from a lot of the other participants, while you're over here you can glance over there and talk to those people and *both* sides of the room feel a sense of closeness to you. Sometimes things go wrong, sometimes you don't have a chance to speak from a stage with full lighting, but you can still get your message across if you're flexible enough and prepared enough to walk into the audience and be a part of the group.

LESSON 24

WHEN OTHERS USE YOUR TIME

What do you do when others run overtime? It's your turn to speak next and they're running into your timeframe. What do you do? Who tells them? Well, I would suggest you have the person in charge of the meeting do the notification. Have them tell them, don't take the initiative to do it on your own unless it's your meeting. But, if you're not in charge of that meeting, if you're just the next speaker, have *them* deal with the problem. If they don't deal with the problem, you can't be held accountable for the lack of time that remains. So, just take what you have to deliver and deliver it within the remaining time and just make it work. That's what professionals do. But, how do you cut, what do you cut? I would say don't cut the main message cut the warm-up. Cut some of the illustrations but get to the point, here is an example.

Deliver a 60 Minute Talk in 19 Minutes?
The Cathcart Method™ - Be Flexible

Years ago, I spoke for the Oklahoma Association of Life Underwriters. It was in Stillwater, and they had speakers all morning long, all day long. I was on late in the morning, we were going into the lunch break after me. All the early speakers had run overtime. All of them. Without exception, all of them. Finally, the guy just before me was really digging into my time and I had about ultimately 19 minutes to do my one-hour speech. Now, what happened was the meeting planner got up there and said, *no, no, don't leave the room yet*. He said, *we've got one more speaker*. Everybody groaned. He said, *"No, you're going to like this guy!"* Then he read my introduction.

Now, I knew I had 19 minutes to deliver a one-hour speech, and everybody wanted to leave because they hadn't had a bathroom break yet that morning and lunch was next. So, I ran to the platform when he finished my introduction, ran, to indicate urgency to the audience. Jumped up on the stage and I said, "*You're about to witness a miracle! You're going to see a one-hour presentation delivered in 19 minutes, get your pencils ready.*" Then, I jumped right into my material. I did 1,2,3,4, hit the points that I was going to make, summarized it, and got off the stage. Got a standing ovation. The people loved it, the meeting planner was thrilled, I made it work. I was able to pull that rabbit out of the hat, thank heavens but a lot of times we're not that prepared.

Know in advance that these sorts of things happen. There will be occasions where you'll have to do something like that. Focus in those cases on the effect you want to have not on the content you want to deliver. It's not about your speech material, it's about how your speech affects the audience that day.

So, look at the time frame, cut out what isn't absolutely essential to the message, deliver that message with conviction and then get off the platform. You and the audience will all be happier because of it.

LESSON 25

KNOW WHEN TO SMILE

Here's a quick one, remember when to smile. Smile when others are looking at you. When you're a professional speaker, when you're the key event at a meeting, when you're the next on stage, everybody is looking at you. Should you smile throughout the speech? Should you sit up there with a false smile and give them that? No. What you should do is just recognize that when you smile you're more appealing. When you smile, you've got more charisma. When you smile, whether there's something funny or not, the smile enlivens your face. It brings a little sparkle to your eye. So, remember to smile whenever you're doing your presentation and cultivate the habit of having a natural smile about you.

Even when your speech is not at all funny, if you pleasantly smile throughout the presentation it will have a positive effect on the audience. I remember a friend whose child said to him one time, hey, dad, are you angry? He said, no, I'm not angry. Why? He said, well, your face looks angry. If you're in a bad mood, don't share it with the audience. Let the smile shine through. If you're in a good mood, for heaven sakes, show it visually.

LESSON 26

WHERE TO LOOK DURING YOUR SPEECH

Where do you look during your speech? Do you look at your notes? Do you look at your audience? Do you look at the slides there on a screen? Where do you look? It varies one person to the next. What I recommend you look at most is your audience. It's okay to look at the other things, as long as that doesn't become a distraction. You know, they say in retail that the most thanked thing in the world is a cash register. Think about that. You go into a store, a person's processing all these people there at the cash register. They're ringing up sales, they say thank you very much, next. They thanked not the person but the cash register, for heaven's sake. If you want to say thank you to somebody, look them in the eye.

Where do you usually look? Get into the habit of noticing where you typically look when you're giving a speech.

I found that I tended to look at one side of the room more than the other. By noticing that, over two or three speeches, I was able to correct that and spend more time with each of the sections of the audience. If you can divide an audience, in your mind, into four groups then you have center-left, center-right, far left, far right. As you look at the audience, you can alternate your attention from one to the other. I would say, don't go 1234-4321 because you'll just look like a robot or a windshield wiper. Instead, look at this section of the audience for a little while and then glance over here and talk to them and then over here and talk to them and then over there and talk to them so that there is variety in what you're doing.

It seems more natural. It may not feel natural until you get used to it but it will seem more natural to the audience.

Don't succumb to the temptation to look just at the people who are intensely listening to you. Look at them, of course. Get that encouragement from them but also look at the other people and spread your eye contact around so you're able to reach everybody in the room. Especially, if you've got someone in the room that's angry or distracting or annoyed or somehow giving you bad messages, do not focus on that person. You might notice him once or twice but do not allow them to occupy your focus because it will show up in how you speak. It'll get you upset. Alternate who you're looking at and how you look at the audience and remember, if you look at your materials, just glance at them long enough to get information; not long enough that you could be considered talking to the screen, to the notes, or to where there aren't people.

LESSON 27

HIT YOUR MARKS

In theater, they tell you hit your marks. That means when you come out on the stage, step to the space where you are supposed to be because that's where the lighting and everything is set for. Deliver your lines from that spot, from your mark on the stage. A lot of times they'll literally have a mark, like a little taped x that's down there on the floor so that you know where your spot happens to be.

Well, in a speaking environment the same thing is true. Learn where your marks are. Learn beforehand, before the meeting ever commences, where the spot is going to be or spots are going to be, where the lighting is best so that everyone in the room can see your face and see your gestures. When you step onto the stage, deliver your message from there. Now, I'm not saying you can't move around but if you know where the light is you can use the light as a tool in your speaking. If you're making a point that doesn't require a great deal of light (you show a lot of energy, you got a lot of stories involved in it) tell it as you move, tell it from any spot in the room. But, when you want to deliver a punchline or when you want to do some kind of a gesture that has meaning, do it in the best possible spot. Use the light.

Sometimes that's center-stage, sometimes is not.

A lot of times, though, what will happen is the meeting crew - thinking that if you're going to have slides or some kind of visual, they think that's the main show and the speakers are just support, just narrators - they will set up the room so that everybody can see the slides clearly, but they can't see the speaker very well. Well, in the past, that's the way presentations like that were done. But, for a professional speaker, most of the time you are the main audio-visual. You're the show. Reset the room or make your request early enough in advance so that it doesn't have to be set wrong in the first place. So that the center of the stage in front of the room is that spot for you with all the light that you need, and the slides are projected onto a screen off to one side or the other or they're on a large screen up above your head so that you're not standing in the projection from the slide projector.

You are the Show! You are the Speaker

Also, if you walk onto the stage and there are two lecterns, be sure you know which one you're going to go to before it's time to get on the stage. Sometimes your introducer will be at one, you'll walk up to the other one to begin your speech. Other times, your introducer will be at the one that you are expected to speak from. Find out in advance. By the way, if you are ever an introducer, when you're on the stage and you finish the introduction, wait until the speaker gets there before you leave the stage. Don't leave the audience looking at an empty room, stand there and wait for the speaker to get to the front. Shake his or her hand, wish them well, and then step quietly off the stage. If you're the speaker, as soon as you get onto the stage, don't just ignore your introducer. Wave to them or shake their hand and thank them and then begin your introduction, your own personal speech introduction. Whenever you're moving on a stage, have a reason to go where you go. Know where the marks are, hit your marks.

GREETING DIFFERENT AUDIENCES

Good morning, ladies and gentlemen, Bonjour, Buenos Dias, Guten Tag, Ni Hao Ma, Konnichiwa, G'day, and in my native tongue from the American South, *how y'all doing? How're your mama and them?* We run into all kinds of audiences and a different type of greeting is appropriate for each one. Sometimes we get an audience where there's a mixture of cultures. If that's the case then you need to use some form of acknowledgment of each of those cultures, to let them know you know they're there and you respect and honor them. You don't have to spend a lot of time on it, you don't have to come up with all kinds of different words. But, just a little something to show you were paying attention or that you were at least trying. It makes a big difference with the audience; it goes a long way. Now, you also need to recognize and respect that in each setting there's a certain amount of formality or informality that is called for.

If you come on too formal, you'll create a stiffness, an awkwardness with the audience, a disconnect. If you come on too informally then a lot of times you'll lose their respect, and they won't be listening to you as they should. Remember to pay attention to the culture you're getting into and today there are so many sources. You can go to the web; you can go to the Brigham Young University which produces what's called culture grams. It gives you a bio or background of each of the cultures and tells you how they think and what they care about, what offends them and what pleases them, and so forth. But, spend just a little bit of time. Regarding those words that I was using while ago, I sat down with some translators one day and I just asked what's the appropriate way to say good morning, good afternoon, good day to these various people, and they gave me many of those. There are more as well. I carry that list with me when I'm on the road, in the event I encounter some other cultures represented in today's audience.

I remember one time in Hawaii, I give a speech and a man answered or asked a question and I said "good question" then I answered the question. Later, I was talking with someone in the hallway, and he said, *you were rather disrespectful to the questioner.* I said, *excuse me? In what way was I disrespectful?* He said, *you just answered the question.* He said, *in our culture* - and this was a man from I think New Zealand. He said, *we would say, the gentleman asked or…. Thank you sir, and then go on that way.* Different formalities but if you don't know what those are you could be stumbling across problems constantly and not even realize it until it's too late to make a difference. So, pay attention, honor your audience, and understand your audience. Good day.

LESSON 29

KEEPING YOUR VOICE

I went to my friend Danny Cox, who is a professional speaker, one time. I said, Danny, I understand you had problems with your voice one time, and you went to a voice coach? He said, yeah, Gary Catona. Then, he referred me to Gary. Gary Catona is voice coach to a lot of the Hollywood movie stars and some singers as well. Some of the people that he's coached were people who had reconstructive surgery on their voice box like Jack Klugman, who used to play Quincy on television. Jack went through a pretty severe surgery on his voice and almost lost it entirely and Gary helped him rebuild that. Dennis Weaver, who was in the old Gunsmoke series years ago, he worked with him. He worked, of course, with Danny Cox. He also worked with Robert Blake, the infamous actor. One time when I went over to Gary's house for a coaching session, Robert Blake was still there taking his lesson. He worked with Shirley MacLaine. He worked with Paula Abdul, the singer and dancer. What I found from Gary was that the voice is your instrument, and you really have to take care of it in a very specific way.

He taught me a number of techniques for loosening up my vocal cords and for expanding and using my voice more effectively, whatever discipline you want to follow. Whether it Gary Katona's method which he will happily teach – he's in Hollywood by the way - or someone else, find a technique that's done by a proven person who has dealt with people with clinical problems, as well as just business problems related to their voice. Practice those techniques and make it just like a physical warm-up. If you're going to do a workout, you stretch and you do a warm-up first, do the same thing before you speak, get in the habit of it. What I do is each day, if I'm in a hotel before meeting, I will, just after I've gotten ready for my day, I'll take a towel because I don't disturb the neighbors and I'll hold the towel in front of my mouth. I will go through the voice exercises quite loudly and just loosen up my voice. I find that there are far fewer occasions where I find that my voice won't quite do what I wanted to do. It really does help. The more I speak, the more important I found it to be.

One time, I was speaking eight days in a row with a little bit of travel mixed in between. But, eight consecutive, full day seminars doing strategic planning retreats for a number of insurance agencies around the country. By the third or fourth day, my voice was getting weak. The fifth day, I was flying from Kansas City to Seattle. Seated on the aisle, a guy across from me was a novelty salesman who loved to talk. He looked at his seatmate and his seatmate seemed to be asleep so he couldn't talk there. He looked over at me and I was evidently alert because he caught my eye. He said, *how you doing?* I said, *fine.* He said, *great, what do you do? I work as a professional speaker. Well, that's interesting, how did you get into that?* I thought about it. Now, I usually try to be very accommodating and courteous but that morning I realized I had a lot more at stake than just common courtesy. I said, *pardon me, but for the last five or six days, I've been doing all day seminars. I've got a few more of those coming up and I really need to save my voice.* He said, *oh, it's okay* and he started asking some other questions. I said, *excuse me.* I said, *I'll be happy to continue this since I'm a professional speaker. I'll be happy to continue our discussion for a fee but I've got to protect my voice.* He said, *point taken, sorry, thank you.* I was able to rest and relax my voice for the balance of the day. Sometimes you have to be a little more direct than other times.

Some of the things that contribute to voice problems are moisture, lack of moisture. Like, if you're in a real, dry environment like on an airplane, it might help to have a little spray bottle with some water in it, Evian or something, and just use that as a spritzer to, moisten up your vocal cords and your nasal passages while you're on the flight. Also, avoid alcohol and avoid caffeine to whatever extent you can because that's going to dry out your voice. The better you can keep your instrument in tune, the better you can take care of your voice and recognize it's got to be with you the whole distance throughout the entire speech and the whole speaking career, the better you're likely to watch over and take care of that wonderful instrument you were born with.

LESSON 30

WHAT TO DO WITH THE 10 MINUTES BEFORE YOU SPEAK

Here's a quick tip on what to do with the 10 minutes before it's time for you to speak. If there's not another speaker already on the platform, in those last few minutes go up on the platform and double check the details at last. Check to see if your notes are where you want them to be, check to see if you have any props that they're placed in the appropriate location and that they're not seen by the audience until the moment you want to reveal them. Check the lighting, check the sound. Also, whether you can easily get onto the platform or not, check your own microphone. If you're wearing, like I do, a wireless lavaliere microphone then make sure you know where the on-off switch is on the remote, make sure that you've checked/tapped on the microphone to see to it that the sound is coming through appropriately.

Make sure that you're checking yourself, make sure that all your clothing is in order, that you look the way you want to look. Make sure you're in the place you need to be. Make sure that in that 10-minute period that the person who is introducing you sees you and knows that you're in the room and accessible so that when they do the introduction you'll actually step up. Assure that they have a copy of your introduction with them.

Also, check the audience. Look around, look at the setting. See who else is there, what's going on, and just get a general sense of things and then you can settle into your last-minute preparation looking for your path onto the stage, doing your breathing exercises, whatever. But, in those 10 minutes before your speech, double check just about everything you can think off. Check the setting, check your materials, check yourself, check the audience, and get yourself in the right frame of mind. Your speeches will go a lot better.

LESSON 31

ARTICULATION MATTERS

Articulation matters. You ever have someone in your audience saying, hey, what did he say? What did she say? If the people are saying that pretty often, it's probably you who has the problem. We need to be careful how we say the words we say. It's okay to have an accent, you don't need to get rid of your accent but make sure that what you say in that accent is understood by your intended audience. One of the things you can do for this is record yourself. Get some recordings of every one of your speeches and get other people to listen with you and have them point out to you when you fumbled or when you said something that was hard to understand. They say wait a minute, you said sea, did you mean see, S E E, or were you using the letter C? What was your intent there? Have people bring that to your attention and then you can be a whole lot better.

I remember a friend who delivered a very compelling speech but then he started talking about aerobatic fitness. Now, what he meant was aerobic fitness, but he got that one word 'aerobics' wrong and he unintentionally said aerobatics. It ended up in the final recording of his presentation - which was distributed for resale - and he lost credibility with just about everybody who listened to it. Though he was presenting good, accurate material, that one erroneous word ruined his credibility with his listener. Another word "Irregardless" that's frequently used and it's a non-word. It's a word that was made up. Now, regardless, that's a good word. That's a solid word, you'll find that in most of the dictionaries. Ir- regardless is a double negative. It is a word that was created by Al Capp, who is the creator of a comic strip called Lil' Abner.

In Lil' Abner, there was a woman called Mammy Yokum and she was sort of the matriarch that ran the whole show. She would often say "Irregardless" - and it was delivered at first as humor, but it's dropped into common usage in our society. Another is the words... You and I versus you and me.

There are times to use one of those, there are times to use the other. There is a difference. You and I, if it's followed by a verb or could be followed by a verb, probably is the right usage. He did that and he wanted notice of that to be sent to you and me because then you're the subject of it. Study up on that a little bit just enough that you're not making the embarrassing mistakes of using it in the wrong way.

Know what speech mannerisms you have. If you have some little distracting mannerisms find out about them by taping yourself and watching what you do.

A friend the other day was saying to me '*and before you know it,* such and such happened. He continued with his story and then he said, *before you know it.* Five times in this little, short story he was telling me, he used the phrase *and before you know it.* Another is "the fact of the matter is....". You'll hear people use that and things like it over again. Make sure you're not using those techniques in ways that you don't intend to use them. Say it, hear it, and resay it until you say it clearly for all your listeners.

The politician Donald Trump is famous for saying, "I can tell you this" or "I can tell you that." He adds these into an otherwise useful statement that does not need the extra modifications. It is distracting and takes away from his message.

Here's something I got from a friend who is a speech coach. It's called Word Tasting. It comes from speech coach Ron Arden of San Diego, California who also lives half the year in South Africa. In this,

it's an exercise. Here's a quote from Aristotle, "The true purpose of all rhetoric is to persuade and influence." Ron says, learn to taste your words. Here are some examples. He said, here are some words you can practice with, words that sound like what they mean clang, clatter, thump, thud, crash, splash, patter, tinkle, creak, moan, grumble, crackle, flap, fizz, buzz, mumble, murmur, whisper, stutter, pluck, howl. Words that sound like what they mean. The reason for this is just to have an exercise that gets you accustomed to making the sounds in a way that gives them the emphasis they need. Then, he has some others - words that create images and feelings: magnificent, brilliant, delicious, delicate, gargantuan, minuscule, delightful, monumental, lascivious, ugly, gentle, firm. There are lots of words that we can practice with to develop the vocal techniques that allow us to be much stronger every time we're on the platform.

LESSON 32

SEE THE MEETING ROOM
RIGHT AWAY. BE EARLY!

Here is a quick tip, see the meeting room early. When you get on-site for whatever speech you are going to give, if you're part of the program, go to the meeting room where it's going to be held as early as you can. If you have to go around one of the side doors because the main doors are locked while they are doing room set up, just go in and peek at the room and see how is laid out. Get a sense of how high the ceiling is, how the lighting is in the room, how the seating is being arranged, and just get a visual picture and an emotional feeling of what that room is going to be like. You can catch potential problems. If you're there early enough you can arrange some of the resetting of the chairs, if necessary. But, most of all, go in there to get a mental image of what it's going to feel like to be in that room later giving your presentation. It is especially helpful if you can also go up onto the stage and stand there and look around and kind of think through how you will approach the opening portions of your speech. The more clearly it's established in your mind, the more effectively it can be delivered at the time the meeting begins.

LESSON 33

COACH YOUR INTRODUCER

Do you want to make a new friend? Coach your introducer. The person who is assigned the job of introducing you to the audience, sit down with them, get to know them briefly. First, listen to them and find out who they are and what they're interested in. Then, explain to them what you're trying to accomplish in your speech. When you present your introduction to them for them to read or to read from, put them at ease. The chances are good they don't do this very often. It's very likely when they get on the stage, they're going to be nervous. When people are nervous on stage, they can go in any direction under the sun. There is no telling what'll come out.

A lot of times they'll try to get cute or funny and it doesn't work. Sometimes they say really embarrassing things. Sometimes they just get the details wrong. There's a lot of things that could happen. Give them a chance to shine. Write a simple introduction, maybe one that has a laugh built into it. Show them that you respect them, and you appreciate the job they're doing for you. If they feel like they're in a partnership with you to do this introduction, they're less likely to use sarcasm or to put you down or to use something cute and to ruin your introduction. I once had an introducer read a portion of my intro and then roll his eyes and mock what it said! Be sure to make your introducer your friend. They are a lot more likely to show you respect and to do their introduction well. Make their job easy, they're going to like you.

LESSON 34

COACH YOUR CAMERAMEN

A lot of times today when you speak you have cameramen around the room. You have people operating cameras and projecting your image up on onto a big screen or recording the presentation. What I like to do is I go into the meetings early, always, and I meet the camera personnel. I go over and introduce myself to them and I show respect. They're not used to that. Speakers often ignore the crew. Most of the presenters are just "talent." You know, the folks that are going to be up there doing whatever they do. So, in response they think of you as *just talent* or as *the speaker* and there is no sense of a personal relationship.

Create a Personal Relationship

So, when I come into the room, I'll go over, and I'll meet the camera people. I'll introduce myself and I'll ask a little question or something to kind of build some rapport with them, get to know them. Then, I'll say, *Tell me where you need me to be for the best video shots and let me briefly describe how I'm going to present and what I'm going to do so that you can have a better sense of where I'll move and how I'll move. By the way, I'll try to always stay in the light, and I'll try to hit my marks and be where you need me to be. Here's a story that I'm going to tell about halfway in. About halfway in, I'd really like you to pull in tight because my facial expressions are a big part of that story. It's a story about this, this, and this.* You give them a sense of what this story is so they'll know it when they hear it. They'll know to pull the camera in and pick up those facial expressions on the big screen or on the recording.

Double check to see who will be calling the shots for the cameras. It may be another person on the crew who directs the camera people through a headset. You must befriend that person most of all.

Also, you could tell them, *I realize that sometimes it makes it awkward for you when a speaker moves around a lot real fast. So, I'll try and be deliberate with my motions and I'll try not to move too quickly, but I will be moving some. There's one point in the speech where I may come down into the audience, but I'll be sure to only come into the first couple rows. Even though I'm stepping out of the light, I'll just be there for a moment to make a point then I'll go back up on the stage. Please at the end, please make sure that you capture 100%, maybe even 110%, of the audience's reaction at the end of the speech. It would be a real tragedy to have the whole speech recorded and then at the end shut off the camera while the audience is still applauding. It's easy to cut that out in post-production when you're editing after the speech but it's impossible to put it in if you didn't capture the image in the first place. So, please leave the camera running all the way through the entire applause. If there's a large audience, please pull the camera back, open the lens, to get the whole room while they are applauding so that the viewers can see what the reaction is. Then, if you need to come back in tight on the stage to pick up on what we're doing there, you can always do that.*

Also, something I suggest to the camera people is that early in the presentation that they get an establishing shot. Meaning you establish what kind of meeting this is by showing a big wide shot of everyone in the room, the entire stage. The speaker may be tiny in the image, but you start with the establishing shot -maybe during the introduction- and then you zero in on the introducer. Then, you follow the speaker to the stage and stay on the speaker and occasionally pull back to show the audience, back in on the speaker. If you know how this works, if you've learned a little bit about it, you can coach the camera people. Recognizing they're the experts not you. You just want them to understand how you speak and how you need it captured on film or on the big screen. In doing that, you will have a much more effective video projection and a much more useful recording of what you just did.

ENERGY CHECK: MANAGE THE INTENSITY OF YOUR PRESENTATION

Here's a quick tip for managing the impact and the energy of your presentation. Be aware of your energy and pace, what I call your personal velocity, on the platform. Don't be too much of a drone and don't try to be the Master Motivator. Find a place in between those extremes where you can use both of those extremes when you want to use them. If you want your ideas accepted, give your ideas a chance to be accepted. Present the idea and then be quiet. Let the idea sink in, give people a moment to reflect on it. Then, present your next idea. If you want your idea to have a dramatic impact on them, you don't have to wave your arms and do big dramatic things in a loud voice. You can make the same impact by whispering.

Simply deliver the message in a frame where it gets 100% of their attention and there are no distractions. Sometimes you can use high-energy, sometimes not. When should you lower or raise your voice?

When it means something. In other words, don't just use vocal techniques to use vocal techniques. Have a reason for doing it, don't just use movement and energy. Have a reason for doing it. When you do it intentionally, you get the results you are seeking.

LESSON 36

KNOW YOUR PATTERNS

Socrates said, "Know thyself." I've found that people who know themselves grow themselves. People who know themselves make better decisions. People who know themselves are a lot easier to work with. One thing you need to know about yourself as a speaker is your patterns. What are the particular ways you approach things? How do you deal with problems? What kind of problems come up the most often for you? What kind things do you do? What kind of difficulties do you encounter? What works for you, what doesn't work for you?

If you study over time then you'll see that, a lot of times, there is a pattern to those problems and some of those problems are just caused by the simple way that you approach things. For example, you might find that you often have problems with your sound system. Well, maybe it's something you need to learn about the sound system that would make you more effective in dealing with it. Maybe you need to show up earlier. Maybe you need to request a different type of microphone. Maybe you need to understand more about the dynamics of the sound in a room and how you get feedback and why and what to do when you get it. Maybe you have problems with travel. It might be that you're booking your flights too close together or too far apart or maybe you're booking it in the wrong way or you're using a travel agent that doesn't understand the ins and outs of travel. Whatever, study your problems, study voice problems. It might be that you're using your voice in a way that damages the actual voice so you end up with voice problems like hoarseness, and so forth. What about room set up? If you're constantly having trouble getting people to participate with you, maybe by changing the way the chairs are positioned you'd get more cooperation. Little things can make a big difference.

What kind of audiovisual difficulties do you run into? Maybe you should have a different type of technology. Maybe you need a new laptop or remote. Maybe you need a different portion of a particular software or app that you use to make it easier for you to do what you do. Don't limp along when you can get your foot repaired and go right back to normal walking. That applies in all areas. When you're having to make do, way too often, chances are good there's a pattern that you are repeating that needs correction. So, back off every once in awhile and kind of get an aerial view of what's going on with you. How do you approach things? How you deal with things? What kind of things do you encounter? The more you know about yourself, the more you can control, direct, and grow in relation to yourself.

LESSON 37

WHAT TO DO WHEN LARYNGITIS ATTACKS

The speaker's nightmare, laryngitis. What do you do when the voice gives out? Well, I've had it happen. I've been speaking for over 40 years and sometimes doing as many as 123 speeches in a year. A typical year for me has about 30 or 40 speeches in it. I've had a couple of occasions where my voice failed. One of them was in Newport Beach, California. I was speaking to an insurance company the next day and my voice started to get kind of raspy. It wasn't like a sore throat, but it was clearly getting very hoarse. I didn't know what that was about, so I did some exercises with my voice the night before I went to sleep. Went to sleep early, didn't drink any alcohol that night, didn't drink any coffee the next morning but still when I woke up, I had a very weak voice.

So, I called a voice coach friend of mine and had him do an exercise with me over the telephone. That helped a little bit. Then, I went downstairs, and I found that the meeting room I was in was very cold and the coldness was making my voice get worse. As I sat there and listened other speakers, I could tell that my voice was being affected. When I spoke to the person next to me, during one of the quiet moments, the voice was getting weaker. So, I grabbed the meeting planner and I said, *let's go out in the* hall and she went in the hall with me. I explained my problem with the voice. I said, *I'm perfectly willing to get up in front of the group and to go right ahead with the presentation but I want you to realize that my voice has the potential of giving out on me in this presentation. So, let's have a backup plan.* I said, *there's a guy in the audience who I know has a good message and understands this group. Maybe he would be a good backup presenter?* She said, no, actually he presented yesterday. Oh, okay. I said, *well, let me call a friend of mine who lives near here.*

So, I called my friend Danny Cox; Danny lived about 30 or 40 miles away. He answered and I said, *what are you doing?* He said, *getting ready to go out in the garden to do some work.* I said, *wrong uniform, put on a suit, please. Come meet me in Newport Beach* and I him told my problem. He said, okay. He dropped everything, put on a suit, came over to Newport Beach to be a standby speaker, in the event that I couldn't do my talk. Then, I talked with my producer, and I said, *okay, my voice is weak, it might give out, but I'm willing to give it a shot if the audience is willing to go with me. Would you please explain that during my introduction?* He said, *happy to.* He got up there and said our speaker this morning is ..... Read my introduction then he said, *Jim woke up this morning with a raspy voice and it might give out on him. But, if you're willing to put up with kind of a strange sound from him, he's willing to give it a try. What do you say?* Everyone applauded, I got on the stage, and I said in a gravelly voice "good morning." They recoiled – kind of in shock. I said, could we get this out of the way right off? Would everyone please just say, awww, and let's get it over with. They all said, awww, and we laughed. Then, I went on speaking and my voice got a little stronger as it loosened up.

Everything went fine. I was talking about relationship selling and the importance of relationships in our business. I said, *you know, when I knew my voice was failing, I called my friend and my fellow speaker, Danny Cox. Danny drove over here to be on standby in the event he was needed in this meeting. Let me introduce you to Danny Cox.* Danny came up on stage. I said, *Danny tell them your story about such and such.* He stood there for about five minutes and delivered a very good story that was very funny.

The audience loved him. As a matter of fact, the meeting planner booked him for the following year's meeting. He went back down off the stage; I finished my speech; everything went fine.

I went home happy, client was happy, Danny was happy, everything's great. Well, the next morning I woke up mute. I had pushed it over the edge, my voice was gone. Couldn't even whisper very well. So, I woke up - I was at home in La Jolla at the time. I whispered to *Paula.* She said, *why are you whispering?* I said, *I have no voice.* Then, she said, *oh my gosh, you've got a speech in three hours, what are you going to do?* I said, *call Tony*. So, we called Tony Alessandra. He is a good friend and former partner of mine and also a fellow speaker. Paula said, *Tony are you busy today? Can you do a speech this morning?* He said, *ummmm, yeah.* Paula said, *okay. Put on a suit and meet Jim at the Hyatt.* I put on my suit, and I went to the meeting just as if I was ready to deliver the speech, though I had no voice. Tony went with me. Tony and I talked about the speech, about what the assignment was and about his message and how similar it was to mine and how he could deliver a portion of his message and achieve the goals that have been assigned to me.

We got there together, walked up to the meeting planner; I motioned her over. She said, *good morning.* I whispered, *good morning.* She said, *what's that?* I said, *I have a problem and a solution.* She said, *what?* I said, *I have a problem and a solution.* I said, *here's the problem, obviously my voice. The solution is Dr. Tony Alessandra, the author of this book and that book. He knows this and he has my material and he's prepared to deliver the speech if it's okay with you.* She said, *whew, that's a relief.*

Yeah, that would be fine. So, he gave his introduction to the person that was doing that. That person got up on the stage and introduced me so I could introduce Tony. Now, I got up on the stage - and the introducer had just said, *Jim Cathcart's our speaker. Jim's got a voice problem. Jim's back up speaker is Tony Alessandra.* I stood up there and whispered the introduction, as best I could, for Tony into the microphone. It worked beautifully; they were excited about Tony. Tony delivered a great speech. I gave Tony the fee, after all, he earned it. It went well. That's the way it works. So, in this business when you're in a position where you know you're not able perform, get somebody else to be a backup for you or at least meet with your meeting planner immediately when you recognize the problem or the potential problems and develop a backup plan. That's the way the professional speakers deal with it.

LESSON 38

WHEN A/V STOPS WORKING

Some quick tactics for what to do when the lighting or the audiovisual stops working. Get closer to your audience, physically closer, so that they can hear you better and see you better. So that they feel more a sense of connection with you. Add more light in any way you can. Open the drapes and the windows, get doors open. Whatever will bring light into the room and speak more distinctly. Now, it's interesting there's a correlation. Literally, they've tested and proven this. That people, when they can't see you very well, can't hear you as well even if the volume is turned up. There's some connection between our perception visually and our perception audibly that blends those two together at some point. So, make sure that if people can't see you very well that you take time to be more specific, more articulate, more distinctive in what you're saying.

Also, ask more questions because if there's poor lighting or poor sound you need to involve those people. Otherwise, their attention will drift. So, ask more questions of your audience. Get them raising their hands, have groups of people stand up to illustrate one of your points. *How many of you, please stand up...* something like that. Don't focus on the audiovisual problem, that's unprofessional. If you're standing up there saying, okay, you know, we've got to do this and will somebody do that. You're trying to direct things from that stage instead of staying in touch with the audience. Very unprofessional and it looks like you don't know what you're doing. Okay, so focus on the audience, focus on the message, involve them more, and let those who can address the audiovisual problem do that while you do the thing you were brought there to do. Deliver a message.

LESSON 39

ALWAYS GET A COPY OF
THEIR PROGRAM

Whether you speak on the job or whether you speak for a living, always get a digital or printed copy of the program for the meeting you're going to. Why? Because there's no telling what you'll discover. For example, a friend of mine was in a position designed to give a keynote on the subject of listening. So, he prepared his standard listening presentation, the way he wanted to deliver it. He was getting ready to go to the meeting and he got a copy of the program, in advance. He found that every speaker at that meeting was addressing the subject of listening. He would've gotten onto the stage and delivered a presentation that was so similar to many of the other presentations that it would have been embarrassingly redundant, as it was, because he saw that the others were speaking on listening and sales, listening and management, listening techniques for cross-cultural situations, things like that. He was able to weave all of that together and to design a keynote speech that made all of the other speeches seem even more important because of his message. So, if you know that you can do great things. If you don't know that, you can embarrass yourself to death. So, always get a copy of the program because you want to know what's on before you, what's on after you. How does that flow, that material, that information, and that timing flow with what you're going to do? Where's the previous meeting? Are they coming from a remote location to yours? Chances are they might be late, there might be a lot of stragglers, there could be transportation difficulties. Is there a big meal just before your speech? Is there another off-site event?

Jim Cathcart, CSP, CPAE With Jan Payne

See, there are a number of things that could interfere with yours and if you know what's there then you know what the potential problems could be. If you don't know what's on the agenda, it can always sneak up and surprise you in a way that you're not able to recover from it as well as you could otherwise. So, know what's going on. Know about potential overlaps and things like that and even make suggestions for where to put the break, or that sort of thing, to break up the program or allow a little more flexibility for people to move from one site to the next, whatever it happens to be. The more you know, the more prepared you can be.

SECTION 3

LESSON 40

KEYNOTE OR SEMINAR

So, what's the difference between a speech and a seminar or workshop? Well, mostly it's length but it also has a different purpose. A speech is a shorter message. It is designed to change your point of view, to bring you news, to present a couple of ideas, to alter a way that somebody is approaching something. It's a way to touch their hearts or a way to do something that has a broader, bigger context. With a workshop or seminar, you're getting more and more specific because there you are focusing on skills. You're focusing on application. You're focusing on techniques and how to's.

So, if you can think in the overall sense of things that concepts are big and generic. They apply to everything. Strategies are more specific, and they apply to a particular approach. Tactics apply to a specific situation, and functions or operations apply directly to the next action you're going to take. Concept, strategy, tactic, function, or operation. Think that way when you think about a speech or a seminar. In the seminar, you can start with the concept then you want to get quickly into the strategies, the tactics, and the techniques for people. The energy in a seminar is much more flexible whereas in a speech it needs to be high energy. It needs to be kind of bigger than life. In a seminar, you are able to be much more approachable, much more interactive with people.

There is a great deal more involvement on the part of the audience when you're doing a seminar. So, you can have exercises, you can do questions and answers, not at the end but during. You can have people interrupt you, raise their hands and offer to ask a question or provide some input. You can use different techniques but the primary difference between a speech and a seminar is the purpose of the seminar is generally to teach and to practice. The purpose of the speech is generally to inform and to influence.

LESSON 41

GET TO KNOW YOUR SET-UP CREW

There is a group of people who are a part of your speech, and you don't often think about - the setup crew that arranges the meeting room itself. One time in Santa Barbara, California, I didn't make the time to go meet the setup crew and to become friends with them. I walked into the meeting room and there was a fellow in there who was finishing some of the setup. I saw that the room and been set up in a large u-shape. It was for 64 people and yet they had it in a u-shape which is very ineffective for that large of an audience. U-shaped would be good for maybe 18 or 20 people, at the maximum. I needed it set up classroom style. I walked in and I said, *this won't do. U-shaped will not do.* He said, *that's what it says on the chart.* I said, *I understand but it's got to be reset.* He said, *You want it set up? You do-it- yourself.* He left the room.

Now, I had by some choices to make: how are you going to deal with that? I could report him to superiors. I could do any number of things trying to throw my weight around but what was going to happen? Well, it was going to take me longer to get the results I needed. So, I just said to the guy, would you please leave the room? He said, why? I said, because I've got to reset the room and I need privacy. So, my meeting was starting in a few minutes, he left the room, I locked the door. I took off my jacket and tie and I took off my shirt. It was a hot day and I needed to reset the room and last thing I needed was to look like I had just reset a room when I was done. So, without a shirt, I reset the room.

Moved the tables and the chairs around to get it all the way I needed it. Then, I went to the restroom, and I freshened up a little bit. I put the shirt and tie and the jacket back on. Went back in there, unlocked the meeting room door and opened it. About that time, the attendees were coming. I greeted them at the door, welcomed them into the room. The meeting went very, very well. Had I not been there early, I wouldn't have had the chance to reset the room and I would've been stuck with that big u- shape. Had I met my meeting room setup crew and befriended them, I wouldn't have had to do it myself.

One time in Calgary, Alberta, I went into a room that was a long narrow meeting room and it was set up like a tunnel, like a meeting inside a railroad car, with the stage way at the far end and all the long rows coming back. Well, for that room, it was a very ineffective way to set it up. It should been set up with the lectern and the platform on the side of the room and then the people set up in sort of a semicircle around that so that everybody felt close to the stage. So, I went to the meeting setup crew and this time I approached it differently. I said, *"excuse me, you and I are on the same team and currently we've got a problem".* He said, *"what's that?"* I said, *"you know how in the specifications it said to set up the meeting room the way you just did?"* He said, *"yeah."* I said, *well, the client didn't realize what the room was like, and it needs to be set up this way.* I said, *"I realize that's a challenge and you've got other things to do but I'm willing to work with you on this. I'll be happy to help. Could we quickly get this turned around to the other direction? I said, after all, being on the same team, this client's going to judge whether the meeting went well. Not by the speech I gave, not by the setup that you did, but by the combination of the setup and the speech and the catering. They're going to determine whether to come back to this hotel again based on the overall feeling, not just one thing. Shall we get started?"* He said, *sure.* He got some other people, they pitched in. Like that, we had the room turned around. Befriend you setup crew, they can be great assets for you.

LESSON 42

WHAT TO DO WHEN THE FRONT ROWS ARE EMPTY

How you deal with church syndrome? That's what I call it when you walk into a meeting room and you find that all the people are seated 5, 6, 7 rows back from the front row. Huge empty gap at the front between them and the preacher and all the people seated tightly in chairs beyond that one. What do you do when your meeting room fills up like that? When people aren't down front? Well, for one thing, if you wait until you're on stage to do your speech, you've probably chosen the worst moment to do that. What I prefer to do is talk to the introducer or the meeting chairman and just say, *what I'd like to do is assure that there's a better connection between the people on the stage and the people in the audience. We need to fill in those front rows. Would you please ask all the people to stand and then have them all move forward five rows (if that's the number)? They'll be reluctant at first but if you stand there smiling and you look like you expect it, they'll probably do it.* Now, in my experience, that's the case. If the person stands up there and says, *would everyone please stand?* First off, you've broken their inertia, they're not just sitting. They don't sit there and think "am I going to comply or not?" They'll stand. So, you get them to stand, that's a nonthreatening activity.

Then, you say, because there's such a gap between the stage and the audience, would everyone please gather their materials and move forward five rows from where you are right now. You get the people to move forward. Now, if the introducer doesn't handle it and you're stuck with it, one of the ways you can do it is to use humor. Here's something I did a few years ago. I saw that happening several times within one organization, so I printed what I called a first-class upgrade. On an airplane, it's good to get, right? So, I printed up first-class upgrade certificates. I would go into a meeting with several of these in my briefcase.

If I needed them, I would walk into the audience and I would say, you have just been upgraded to first class. I would hand these upgrade certificates to people, and I would say, follow me. The people would grab these, and they'd stand up. I'd lead them back up to the front of the room. Here is what the first-class upgrade says… I just printed up these on my own computer in a Word doc and printed them out on colored paper. You can do the same thing. *"You've just been approved for a full upgrade to first-class seating for the duration of this program. Please move immediately to the designated section towards the front of the room. In conjunction with this upgrade, you will be entitled to a more vital role in the success of this program, quicker responses to your questions and comments, better eye contact with the speaker, longer and better laughs on the humorous parts of the presentation, and more inspiration from the ideas that are presented."* On the flipside, it had terms and conditions. *"Valid only for programs led by Jim Cathcart or any other time you can get away with it. Presenter reserves the right to send obnoxious people back to their original seat. This certificate expires only when you no longer have a desire to learn. Not to be used in conjunction with special group upgrades or in concert with frequent listener programs. If you've read this far, you're not paying attention to the speaker so put this down look up and pay attention. Thank you."*

So, it's something humorous that I did, something that people found playful. It ended up going over very well, it got the job done. So, anytime you've got that kind of a group, you've got several options.

1. Just deal with it and stand up there with that huge chasm between you and them and hope that things go well. By the way, it will be more difficult. Or, 2. step down into the audience and move closer to them and present from what is now the first row, which would be the one five or six back. 3. You can also turn the entire room around. Go back to the back of the room, present from there. People in the back row will now be in the front row. Or, 4. you can just adjourn the meeting for a moment and rearrange the room or remove a certain number of chairs so that when they come back in, in order to find a chair, they have to occupy all the chairs in the room. There are a lot of tactics you can take.

The most appropriate will be the one that's the simplest, gets the quickest result with the least disruption of the audience and the flow the meeting itself. Have some fun with it.

LESSON 43

TECHNOLOGY IS YOUR FRIEND

God bless technology. Boy, it is so much better to be able use something like PowerPoint or Keynote or other apps to make your presentation than it was in the old days when I had to use an overhead transparency or 35mm slides or when I was using only a flipchart or pre-prepared chart to make my points. With things like PowerPoint, there are lots more opportunities and there are also many more challenges. What we must consider is the ways technology can make our job as a speaker easier. Use it in a way that doesn't complicate it and one that makes it smoother and easier to connect and communicate with your audience. Make it serve you. Use your audiovisuals, your technology, the bells and whistles to add drama, to add creativity, to avoid laziness, to get things to keep you on track and from being distracted. When it works for you, it also does the same thing for your audience.

Now, do you sit down and study the manuals and go through classes and learn to use PowerPoint? Well, yeah, that's good but if that's not what you do, if that's not a strength of yours yet, find the experts who do understand it, who can manipulate it, who can use all the bells and whistles and build those in so that they operate automatically, and you don't have to learn those. Then, over time, learn a little a little more a little more a little more so that you can control your own presentation and structure and change and customizing and so forth. Take some online lessons and review the YouTube tutorials. And, for heaven sakes, when you get to a meeting, do your prep before the audience gets in the room.

One of the most embarrassing things in the world is to see a professional standing at a platform, trying to convey the image that you and I try to convey as business people or as leaders, and standing there trying to work out the details of a presentation technology while in front of an assembled audience. That's so unprofessional. Don't let it happen to you. Let the experts build the things for you and you just use them.

When you run into the situation where the crew is handling the advancement of the slides instead of you doing it yourself with a remote, work out your cues in advance. Talk with them about whether you're going to do a hand gesture that indicates next slide, whether you're going to press on button and light up a light back there by their computer to advance to the next slide, or whether you're going to give them a visual or audio cue, where you say next slide please – which kind of distracts.

Email Slides in Advance

Work out the cues in advance and email the slides whenever you can. If you're doing a PowerPoint presentation, email it to the meeting planner in advance and bring it on a thumb drive so that they can load it into their own computer. A lot of times, you can bring your laptop and you could plug it in on stage. But then, you have to have yours plugged in, you have to switch to yours from anything else they're using when it's time for you to speak. You have to undo yours so that the next person can plug in, and it just presents a lot of time delays. So, if possible, email the PowerPoint presentation or whatever it is, to the client in advance.

Bring the presentation on a USB thumb drive as well. Let them load it into their computer so it's just another in a series of presentations they have for the meeting. No need to plug-in and unplug anything and you still have control. You can get there early enough to look at it, go through it, edit it if you want to make some changes. By the way, a lot of times you get to a meeting, and someone will say, hey, just leave your laptop with us and we will work with this, and everything will be fine for tomorrow morning when you speak. Never do that!

Never, Repeat, Never Leave Your Laptop with Anyone Never Overnight

Never, repeat, never leave your laptop, your presentation with anyone, not overnight anyway. You might leave it with them for a few minutes but do not leave it overnight because you're going to lose control. The downside of that is so big and the upside so small. Stay with the people when they're controlling your technology. Stay with them, work with them, and then take your equipment that has the original material in it with you and keep it in your safe care. Technology is wonderful and it gives you lots of possibilities that make things much more fun. Learn to use the technology but don't expect yourself to master it at first. Rely on the other people.

LESSON 44

BECOME THE CHARACTERS
IN YOUR STORY

One of things a lot of speakers use, is what is known as a signature story. And, I have a signature story that's about when I worked as a bill collector. When I was in my 20s, I worked as a bill collector. And, the reason I bring this up is I want for you to learn the technique of becoming the characters in your stories. Here's what I do with the bill collector story. To start out I tell the people that at age 22 I used to be a bill collector. I say, now look at this face. That's me in my 60s, imagine me in my early 20s.

In my early 20s, I had rosy cheeks, none of this gray hair; looked about four years old. Couldn't intimidate my kid sister and what I was doing for a living was repossessing log trucks in the hills of northern Arkansas. And then, I tell the story about going back into the woods and finding these log trucks and here's one of the scenes. I say, *I pulled up near the truck. I walked out of my car over to the truck. Looked up at this big old truck and a hair covered creature climbed down out of the cab. I look him square in the chin and I said, (in a high-pitched scared voice) I'm here to get your truck* - which always generates a laugh from the audience. And then, I switch posture (you notice that I'm moving sides) and I start looking down as if I'm this big character that just came down out of the truck. And, I'm looking down at me like Goliath to David. And I say, *boy, do you realize we're alone in these woods?* and I'd say, *yes sir and I'm leaving now and I'm going back to my car.* As I tell this story, you'll notice, I've moved into the posture of each of those characters. I assumed a big posture looking down and looking in that direction when I was the past due logger. And, when I was the little bill collector 22 years old, I was looking up and I was taking more of a meek posture and even showing weakness in my voice. There was a voice difference between the way I played each character.

The Cathcart Method™ Movement for Meaning

In another story that I tell, I talk about being in a McDonald's and having a dialogue with a woman nicknamed Grandma who worked at McDonald's. And, when I'm speaking, I'm holding the tray and talking to her. And, when she's speaking, I've changed my posture little bit and I act as if she were standing behind the counter and not holding the tray. There are little **visual cues** that let the listener know that you've changed from one character to the other. Because as far as they're concerned, for the moment you're telling about that character, you are that character. So, if you can somewhat slip into the role of that character without trying to do dramatic acting and just use a few of the little theater techniques that add some drama to that or add some vividness to the illustration, then you make your point with them far more powerfully. Don't try to become an actor unless you're trained for it but do ***get into character*** as needed.

It's like the simple difference between moving while you talk and standing as you deliver a point. A very dramatic difference. It's like a difference in vocal technique and it's visual in this case. So, become the characters in your stories. Use that **The Cathcart Method™ (Be Intentional)** technique, use movement for meaning. Use behavioral patterns, use gestures to comply with the character that you're speaking from, the voice that you're using at that particular time. The more you can do that, the more effectively you can bring those characters to life and cause that audience to remember the story and the point behind it long after you told it.

LESSON 45

GETTING YOUR AUDIENCE IN THEIR SEATS AFTER A BREAK?

How do you get the people back into the meeting room? When they go on break or they go to lunch, how do you get them into the meeting room? You can use sights, you can use sounds, you can use actions, you could have a sign, have somebody say the meeting is beginning, you can have someone dinging a bell, you can have someone clinking a fork against a glass to get their attention, you can have someone walking around notifying everybody that the meeting's beginning, please come back inside, you can do something over the loudspeaker. A lot of things you can do like that.

What I like to do is have several people - if it's a large group - go out into the group and just gently and tactfully herd them back into the room. Just go to the edges of the meeting, down the hallway, recruit a few helpers and say the meeting is starting right now, let's go on back inside and have them guide a few people in. When you see that coming from three or four different locations, no matter where you are in the group, you tend to follow the group and go back in the room.

Set the Expectation

Something else you can do is set the expectation - when you adjourn to the break or to lunch or whatever it is - set the expectation that you're going to have the meeting start exactly on time. If you say, we're going to take a break until 3 o'clock and we'll start the meeting up exactly at 3 o'clock so please be seated at that time instead of wandering back this way at that time. And then, thank them. See you back here at exactly 3 o'clock. Then, at 3 o'clock start speaking! At 3 o'clock, a lot of people say, they're not all back yet, let's wait for the other people. No, they know the rules. They're adults, they made a choice. Reward the people who came back, the ones who are there on time and start the meeting at exactly - if it's 3 o'clock - at exactly that time.

Another thing you can do is you can start the speech when you're starting back up, start it with material that's not absolutely vital to your message and has high-energy possibilities. Like, you might tell a story - a short story – that's got a lot of energy and movement in it that will capture their attention. That will allow you to tell something that's entertaining these people or informing these people while the others drift back in the room. And then, when you get into the main meat of your message, once again, and everybody is seated, and everything is going fine. I saw Zig Ziglar down in New Orleans years ago at a national speaker's convention. And, he adjourned the group to a break for a few minutes and when it was time to come back, somebody made the announcement out in the hallway, the meeting is starting. And, within just a couple of moments after that, Zig launched on to the stage high energy presentation telling a story. He continued to tell that story until everybody got back in the room, delivered his punch line, got a big laugh, and then jumped right back into the flow of his material.

LESSON 46

BEFRIENDING YOUR TRANSLATORS

We live in a global society and more and more all of us are encountering people who speak different languages than we do. We're going into meetings and we're giving presentations, many times, many members of the audience speak English as a second language or maybe not all. In that case, a lot of times the meeting planner will have provided translators. People will sit there with headphones, and they will be listening to another person trying to interpret what you've been saying at the same time that you're saying it. Something I found to be very effective and something I found that is very rare to find done is for the speaker to meet with the translators before the meeting.

What I like to do is find the translator in advance. Maybe I've got a person speaking Japanese, one speaking Spanish, one speaking French, one speaking Italian, one speaking German.

I had one who was speaking a Malaysian dialect, I've had a number of different ones. I sat down with the group, and I said, *let me explain to you how I speak and what I'm speaking about and here's an outline that I've made for each of you, of some of the points I'm going to cover.* So, I gave them a copy of the outline my speech. It wasn't a script because I don't script my speeches and it was a number of points that it was obvious I was going to cover. They could see with my slides I was using; they could see - with the slides - where I was going next. So, I gave them this material and I said, *let me talk about what I'm going to do. There's one story that I'm going to tell that might have a different meaning in some other cultures than it has in mine. Here's the message of the story, here's the purpose of the story, and here's the joke - if there's a joke inside the story. This is why people laugh at this particular point.* These people loved it. They said, *speakers never tell us this stuff, wow.*

Honor Your Audience in Their Language

Then, I said, *what are some phrases or some words I could use that would help the Japanese people, for example, understand that I'm honoring them, that I care about the fact that they're there?* And, they gave me a couple of phrases to say. How can I say good morning in Malaysian? How can I do this in Spanish or French, whatever?

So, I learned from them how to customize my speech a little bit and they learned from me how to customize it a lot. And, in doing so, I showed **respect** to them as the translators, we were fellow presenters, and I talked with them that way. I said, you and I are giving this presentation together. I did this in Venezuela, in Poland and all over the world. So, let me give you a clue as to what I'm going to be doing and why and then you can understand how to best present that because I need what you do. Be a good friend to your translators, they will be a good resource for you.

Respect and Like Your Translator

I often speak in mainland China, with a translator standing beside me on stage translating each paragraph one at a time. This is done even for 2-day programs in front of thousands of people. At first it is very awkward, and once you and your translator become comfortable partners in presenting it can go very well. Most of all though, assure that you respect and like your translator. The audience will too, and they'll admire you for doing so.

LESSON 47

THE CATHCART METHOD™ (BE THOUGHTFUL)
THINGS TO THINK ABOUT

What happens once your speech is over? Are they going to go to a workshop? Are they going to adjourn for the afternoon? Are they going home from the meeting? Do the buses pull up to the front door and everybody piles into the buses and grabs their luggage? Do they go play golf? What's going on after your speech? You see, what's going on after your speech gives you some ideas of what you can do in your speech.

Because, if you know they are going into a workshop then you need to provide them with something tangible so they can remember your points before they go into another presentation to learn yet another set of points. If you know that they're going to play golf or something like that say, "while you're out on the golf course this afternoon, let me give you a couple of things to think about and talk about." You plant some seeds for their discussion later on. If where they're going is home from the meeting, say, *when you get back home you know it's going to be really easy to set these ideas aside and to focus on the day-to-day worries. Here's a way to incorporate this into your continuing life so that it pays off for you after the meeting itself.* The speech should be kind of like graduation from high school. It's not an end, it's a commencement. It's the beginning of the application process.

The learning process may have concluded for that speech and the application process is just beginning for these people. So, give them some guidance on how to continue the growth, give them some tips, give them some tools like books, handouts, materials, articles, reminder cards - things like that. Give them suggestions of specific things they can do. Start the dialogue between the people. Lead them to your website and have some resources for them there. Whatever it takes, give them something easy to use, simple to understand that continues the learning when you're done speaking.

If the next activity is more exciting to them than your presentation then you'll need to plan accordingly if you want their full attention. For example, what if after your speech they are going to Disneyland?

Chances are good that they are thinking more fondly about that trip than your talk. So be livelier, be brief and clear, make it OK for them to be anticipating Disneyland and still make your message valuable to them.

LESSON 48

WHO SHOULD YOU THANK?
(BE GRATEFUL)

In my business career, some of the best times I've ever had were the times when I stopped to thank the people who helped me get to where it was that day. I did that at my 10-year business anniversary, my 20-year, and again at my 25th. I found that it just made me feel wonderful while I was making them feel good about the contributions they had made. Well, you can apply that same principle when you give a speech. Who should you take time to thank for making that speech a success?

For example, the meeting planner who put all the work into making that meeting what it is. What about the people who handle the logistics of the meeting? What about the people that provided information to you in advance? Maybe you interviewed a few of the people to find out about the group or about their needs or to help you with your speech. If you take time to acknowledge some of those people at the appropriate point during your speech, you will not only build your own good feelings you will build their esteem. You will cause them to be respected more by their peers. You will give them a moment in the spotlight. In a lot of cases, you will win their undying support. You can take time to thank the speakers bureau. You can take the time to thank the client. You can thank your staff. Find out who it's appropriate to thank in that setting. Do more than you need to do. Do enough to put some special emphasis on them because more people than just you will always be involved in order for you to be able to have a very good speech.

LESSON 49

BE A LOW MAINTENANCE SPEAKER

Several years ago, I was looking over the contact records between us and our clients in my office. And, I noticed that we had many, many, many phone calls to each client – like 9, 10, 12, 15 phone calls between the first contact and the day of the meeting. I called my staff together and I said, what is this? How come we have so many phone calls? They said, Well, we have to confirm travel, we have to confirm shipments. We have to confirm all these various things. I asked, couldn't you do that in one or two or three phone calls? Well, sometimes it's....I said, let's just back off and take a look at where we fit in the world of the client, okay? I think we need to know our place in their meeting. I said, "This is *their* meeting. What's going on in their meeting?" Well, for one thing, logistics. They have all the details of the meeting, all the materials they have to ship to the meeting, all the room set-up, all the decorations, all the gifts and things that are being given out to the people. They have travel for the meeting. They have all these people that have to get there, and they've got to coordinate that travel, they've got to know when those people are coming.

They also have what you might call VIP experiences and details of the meeting. They have to deal with the celebrities. They have to deal with the company executives, the industry speakers, the visiting dignitaries, the press - things like that. You might add press as a separate issue if that's relevant to a particular organization. They also have to deal with catering, that's a huge responsibility. They have to handle all the food and all the timing of all those things. Then, they have to handle the breaks for the meeting. They've got the lodging for the meetings. They have the audiovisuals, and it goes on and on and on. This thing just gets bigger and bigger and bigger and somewhere in all of this is you the speaker. Somewhere in the mix of all this complexity.

I said to my staff, "In light of the fact that we're just one person and their meeting is a huge complex responsibility, how many phone calls should we require them to return in order for their meeting to go smoothly and go well?" They said, well, good point. We should not be a thorn in their side. They got so many people to deal with, the last thing they need is a high maintenance speaker. So, we started looking at all our processes - that we followed in our office - to deal with each of our clients for an upcoming meeting. We streamlined them and made it a lot simpler and a lot smoother and became less of a burden on the meeting planner and a lot more desirable as their repeat speaker. Be a low maintenance speaker.

LESSON 50

THE SPECIAL OFFER
FOR YOUR AUDIENCE

God bless the Internet. Boy, I'll tell you, we've got the greatest resource and websites. I used to have a printed almanac that was published each year. It was called, Everybody's Business Almanac. It was the equivalent of a mini-internet for each of the major companies in the world. It contained the history of the company in one paragraph, their current stock performance and profitability of the company, the number of offices they had, who's holding the key offices within the organization - things like that. We can go to a website today and learn that and many, many, many times more about any of our clients.

Well, that's good for us in preparation for a speech. We need to also have our own website functioning that way for the people after our speech. We need to offer value on our website. For my website, I was fortunate enough to get the name Cathcart before anyone else in the family did, so Cathcart.com is my own personal website and my business website. On there, I have a number of resources for people. But people won't know that unless you provide that information to them, and you let them know what's there and why they should go to your website. And, I think you ought to provide in writing either in your speech notes or in whatever way is appropriate to the setting, the specific address of the website.

I tell people during the speech, if you would like a copy of the item I just read then there is a reprint of that on my website. Just go to articles, click on this keyword, and you can download it for free. And then, at the end of my speech - a lot of times - I'll have a slide that says, on the website 3 free articles that you'll enjoy: 11 ways to expand your life this year. 21 ways to grow sales this year. 15 ways to grow your business this year. Or I might lead them to video lessons. I just reinforce that this is free material and what happens is you get people continuing the learning process by going to your website. You can also make available your speech notes. Just say, send me an email to Info@Cathcart. com and just say speech notes. I'll know that it's from this audience and I'll send you a copy of the PDF file, which is a photograph basically, of the slides that they can keep and read on their own. It doesn't give them the ability to do the same slide presentation or to use the slides in their own talks and yet they certainly have that material available to them in the PDF file. So, if we can just make our website a tool that extends our speech, a lot of times that'll be just what the audience needs to continue the learning process.

LESSON 51

MEETING ROOM DISASTERS AND RECOVERY STRATEGIES

One of the most popular articles I ever wrote was one years ago entitled, Meeting Room Disasters I Have Known. I talked about the kind of messes that you run into when you're on the speaking circuit and some of the tips that you could keep in mind for recovering from them. I have run into everything under the sun, and it all boils down to kind of a simple list. You can look at the source of the problem: where it comes from like no light, not enough light, not enough sound. Maybe the microphone stopped working or there wasn't a microphone there. By the way, here's a quick tip, if a client ever asks you, do you really need a microphone? Say, no, no, I'll hear it all and if you expect the audience to be able to hear it, you might want me to have a microphone. Sarcasm intended. Microphones aren't for speakers; they are for audiences. Another thing you might have is no audience or wrong audience or not a big enough audience or too big of an audience, no introduction or wrong introduction, audiovisual goes bad or they had the wrong audiovisual. Maybe another speaker didn't show up or you ran out of time or the climate, the environment, is wrong – something is wrong with the setting.

Years ago, I was doing a series of sales rallies for Century 21 Real Estate. This was back in the late 1970s early 80s. I was in Ohio and my host was a guy named Roy McKinney. Roy and I've been from city to city, we've done a number of events. Just before the speech in Toledo, he went up and he took a nap and then he came downstairs. Now, when you take a nap, a lot of times, you're not completely awake in the first few minutes after that nap. So, he came back to the meeting room, and he was still kind of groggy from his nap and he got up to give my introduction. There are several hundred people in the audience: exciting atmosphere.

He started talking about how exciting this tour had been, all these sales rallies. He said, *I've been traveling with our speaker for days and what a guy he is. He started rattling off these things about me that he thought were impressive and valuable to that audience. He said, and now here he is....and at that point he* completely went blank on my name. Forgot who I was. I mean, he clearly knew who I was, and he forgot my name and I saw that he was stuck. Rather than let the minute really be awkward, I decided to make it fun. So, I jumped up out of the audience and I ran to the stage and like I was play acting that we were solving a problem together. I said, *look I've got it here somewhere* and I went through some papers. I pulled out a little brochure that had my picture on it. I said, *there it is, there it is, Jim Cathcart!* He said, *yes, ladies and gentlemen, Jim Cathcart.* And, they all laughed, and they applauded, and I went on and gave my speech just as if we had planned it that way. Well, whew, we dodged a bullet on that one. But, if I hadn't been ready to do something like that, I wouldn't have thought to do it. So, it is good for you to have that kind of consciousness as to what would I do if?

What are the options? How do we do this without taking ourselves too seriously?

One time I was in San Francisco and my meeting planner got called into another meeting and he couldn't come back to our meeting in time to introduce me to speak. So, I'm in the meeting room, it is a small group like 18 people, and I'm going be doing a sales seminar and they don't know what I'm there for.

All they know is there's a sales meeting. They come down to the meeting room. They're sitting there, I'm sitting there, and the host never shows up. It's time for the meeting. A couple minutes go by, I finally decided well, what the heck? They're here for a meeting. I'm the meeting. I might as well as introduce myself. So, I stood up and I said, good afternoon, thanks for being here. Our speaker today

.... And I literally read my own introduction. I said, *"so, let's welcome Jim Cathcart".* Then, *I turned around and I turned back, and I said, "thank you very much for that introduction". Now, that was a very playful approach and there are some settings where that wouldn't work. But, in doing that they all got a laugh and I said, "Leo's not here. He's coming I'm sure, but something has detained him so let's get on with the meeting anyway."* And, they were fine with it and it went well.

Another time, I drove 130 miles one way to a meeting. Got to the meeting, one guy showed up. One guy. The guy who was running the meeting. He had done a poor job of getting the word out about the meeting and the people who would've come didn't come. Now, this was a time when I was not a professional speaker. I was on the staff of the United States Junior Chamber of Commerce. I was in charge of their leadership training programs. So, this guy, his name was James. He had come to the meeting but nobody else came to the meeting because James didn't do a very good job, well, didn't do a good job at all of promoting the meeting. So, I said *okay James, have a seat. You're the district director for this area, I'm going to give you this seminar and then I expect you to take it out to those people that were supposed to be here.* He said, *okay.* So, I did a one-on-one training and taught him how to do the presentation I was going to do and he took it out to the other Jaycees organizations.

One time I was in Minneapolis, another meeting room disaster, or near disaster. It was in a downtown hotel, and they set up the meeting - because the hotel was full of other meetings - they set it up around the swimming pool. So, that the tables were all at one end of the pool and a few tables were even wrapping around the edges of the pool. But, they set up the head table - back in the days when head tables were more common - they set it up so that the people at the head table, when they back their chair up, were backing their chair up within inches of falling into the pool. Now, if you've ever been in an indoor pool you know that that's like a sound studio with the poorest possible acoustics. Everything echoes and sure enough that was the case. This was a horrible place to hold a meeting because anything anyone said was echoed throughout the whole room. I saw what was going on, I realized that the people at the head table could potentially back their chair up too much by accident or step around behind someone else's chair by accident and fall into the pool. So, I took the initiative - even though I was a guest speaker - to inform everyone else that I could about that potentiality. We made some minor adjustments that made it a little bit safer. Then, when they started the meeting, I had them make some comments about the acoustics and to enlist the audience's support in compensating for the bad meeting room. Then, when it was my turn to speak, I stepped out from behind the head table and spoke sort of theater-in-the-round, among the group, and it went well.

One time I was in Florida and the client, I could overhear him - I was there early for my speech about two hours, three hours early. The client was really distressed, and he was talking to someone else. I said, *what happened?* He said, *our next speaker is still stuck in Boston in the airport, he's not going to be here.* I said, *wow, he waited kind of late to call. He said, yeah, what are we going to do?* I said, *put me on.* He said, *"But your speech isn't for like two hours."* I said, *"I'm ready. You do the introduction, I'm ready right now."* He said, *"Man, you just saved my neck!"* He put me on and I did that presentation. Then, there was a short break between that session and the one I was going to do. I went down, put together a second presentation that explored some of those ideas a little further and did a second presentation. No extra charge. The client liked it so much and was so relieved that I'd saved him from that disaster that he booked me for yet another speech.

One time I was speaking of Boca Raton, and I was scheduled for a one-hour speech and I was loaded for bear, wired for action. I was ready to get up there and give the best speech I had ever given. I mean, I really was prepared. Had it all down, knew exactly what I want to do. The client came over and said, *the previous speaker is running overtime and I don't know what to do?* I said, *just motion to him and if he doesn't pick up on those motions then walk up to the stage and say thank you very much, we've got to end this speech. We've got another presentation.* He said, *no, I don't want to do that.* So, the client didn't want to interrupt this guy who was obviously running way over time. He kept running overtime. He ran 40 minutes overtime; 40 minutes overtime! My one-hour speech is now a 20-minute speech.

The guy said, *can you cut it to 20 minutes?* I said, *yeah, but it won't be the same speech. It will be a little piece of what would've been that speech.* He said, *that's okay.* So, I got up and I gave one piece of my three-part speech and that one piece worked very well and the audience didn't know that the other 40 minutes had not been delivered. So, when you've got to cut your material just remember they don't know what you got to cut.

Another disaster, one time we were in the basement of a church years ago, in Dermott, Arkansas. A little rural community, we were in the basement of a church, about 40, 50 people are there. Air- conditioning is broken, it's the middle of the summer. It is so hot, people are melting. They're all dressed up for the event and I'm about to be introduced to speak. So, I was sitting there thinking what can I do? What would I do if I were in the audience, and I didn't care about protocol, but I just wanted to be comfortable? Then, I thought, I've got an idea. So, I went over to the buffet line where they had a little snack before the meeting. And, I picked up a stack of paper plates. When I was introduced to speak, I passed the paper plates all down each side of the room and I said, *Please take a paper plate. hold it at arm's length from your head and on the count of one bring it back your shoulder, on the count of two put it back in front of you. Would you do that? One two, one two, I smiled and said, go-ahead and fan yourself, it's hot as blazes in here. Just make yourself comfortable and use that to keep yourself cool.* They laughed, they enjoyed it, we went on with the meeting. So, any time you're in a situation where everything seems to fall apart, just remember why you're there. Remember that they're experiencing it too. So, don't try to ignore the problem, address the problem. Feel free to do something creative or playful because if you can help alleviate the problem, if you can help that meeting planner be a little more effective in dealing with what's come up, you're going to come out as the hero in the audience is going to love what you had to say.

LESSON 52

GETTING STARTED
AS A SPEAKER

If you truly want to become a professional speaker then, how do you get started as a speaker? Well, in 1974 - I was getting started as a speaker. I used to sell Earl Nightingale's motivational recordings and I went to a conference in Phoenix where one of the people at that conference was Bill Gove. Bill Gove was the first president of the National Speakers Association. I asked, what do I need to know to get started as a speaker? I'm already out there selling materials and doing some presentations, but I want to do what you do for a living. He told me a story about when *he* got started as a speaker.

He went to a conference, and he heard Dr. Kenneth McFarland, one of the great orators of the last century. And, Dr. McFarland had just delivered a brilliant oration and Gove went up to him and he said, Mr. McFarland, Dr. McFarland, I would like to do what you do. I want to be a speaker more than anything in the world. And, McFarland looked at him and he said, you want to speak? Then speak; that was it. You might think, that's kind of lame. I mean, hey, give me more information. I mean you want to speak, speak? Duh. No, actually that was good advice because what he meant was get out there and start giving speeches. If you want to speak, if you want to build a speaking career, get out there and start giving speeches. You might say, but where? Who's going to pay me? That's not your worry yet.

When you're getting started as a speaker, the first thing you've got to do is just start giving speeches. Any opportunity you get, anytime there is a group together that there's a reason for you to be in front of them sharing some ideas, get out there and speak. What's needed is to develop your message, you've got identify your market, and you've got to get some mileage.

Write your Stories

The message: there are a lot of things you could talk about. You can talk about your life. You can talk about your expertise. You can talk about current events.

There are a lot of things to talk about. What you have to determine is what is your message and who cares whether they hear that message or not. So, develop your message, start making notes. Just write down all the stories, all the ideas, all the things that are of deep concern to you that you'd like to talk about. The things that you think you know that others would benefit from knowing. Write those down and just have as many pages of that as you can generate so that you can look back over it and determine what is your message over time. I mean, it's not going to just pop to the top. It will take you a little while to cultivate this.

Then, second look at who's your market? Who are the people who need to know or would like to know what you've got to say? That'll take some time, identifying whether it's a business market, whether it's a specific industry, whether it's people in education, whether it's young people, older people, make it clear.

The next thing you need to do is get some mileage. Now, when I say get mileage I mean you're not going to be a really good speaker until you've been in a number of really bad speaking situations. You got to go out there and speak in a room where the heat gets stuck and everybody's dying of too much heat. You've got to go out there and speak in a room where it's freezing, and you can't get the heaters to work and everybody in there shivering. You got to go in the rooms where the lighting is bad, where there is too much noise in the next room, or the guy who was speaking before you just went 30 minutes over time and ate up most of your speaking opportunity, where the people that came into the room were in an awful mood because of something bad that happened and they're all upset when they sit down to start listening to you. You've got to go speak in places where your introducer doesn't have a clue who you are and gives you a lame introduction and you have to figure out how to recover from that.

See, it's easy enough to be a good speaker and is not easy to be a good speaker when the circumstances aren't good. That's why mileage is so important if you expect to be a professional speaker. People say, well, no. I've got a lot of business experience. I've been out there in the trenches. I've got a message; and the world needs what I've got to say. I'm ready and I'll start charging fees to speak. Well, give it a shot, good luck. Remember it's not what you know that makes you a good speaker, it is your ability to connect with an audience in such a way that they want to listen to you.

My belief is the way to start in speaking today is to join the National Speakers Association. Start going to some of their local meetings, go to some of the national meetings, read their publications, go to their website (nsaspeaker. org), get some recordings of some of the materials and some of the programs they've done in the past. Start learning about the speaking industry and then every time somebody gives you an opportunity to speak, take it. Get out there and speak. Figure out how to be relevant to all different types of audiences, how to connect with people who don't necessarily feel a connection yet with you. As you develop your skill, as you develop your message, as you identify the market, as you get that mileage, your speaking career will take off.

GETTING KNOWN

How do you get known in the speaking industry? How do you establish a reputation? Well, first off, you've got to understand what the speaking industry is. The speaking industry today is comprised of several elements. You have other speakers and those would be found easiest at that the National Speakers Association, the gatherings of that organization and its Global Speakers Federation affiliates. Then, you have MPI, Meeting Professionals International. You have ASAE, the American Society of Association Executives. You have ATD, the Association for Talent Development, Toastmasters International, and The International Association of Speakers Bureaus. All kinds of organizations that comprise the speaking and meetings industry. How you get known in that industry?

Well, the first thing is to get active in the industry. Get out there and do some things. I don't mean just give speeches; I mean get active in the industry. Attend the meetings, be a good audience member, get involved with the people, meet some of the people, attend some of the social events. Subscribe to their websites. Listen to podcasts. The trouble with a lot of speakers is they want to get known in the industry without adding any value to it. They go to the meetings to tell about themselves. That's the quickest way to get known in the industry in a way you don't want to be known - somebody who only wants to talk about him or herself.

To get known in the industry, **get involved** in it, attend the meetings, get to know some of the people, and be a worker not a taker. Offer to help out with a meeting, offer to do an introduction, offer to help straighten up a meeting room, or whatever. Most of all, be involved so that the other people can see you're genuinely there to contribute not just to take something away.

Get Clear on How You Want to be Known

Then next, if you want to be known, how you want to be known? Here's a thought, do a little exercise and ask yourself, how would I like to be known five years from now? What would I like my friends to think about me and say about me five years from now? Just write down one little paragraph of what you'd like them to think and say about you five years from today. Then, think about your colleagues, the people in the business, the people that you know and want to know better. How would you like them to think about you and what would you like them to say about you five years from today? What about your neighbors? What would you like them thinking and saying about you five years from today? What about the clients that you deal with or want to deal with? What would you want them thinking and saying about you five years from today? And, what about the people within the industry - whatever industry you are pursuing? Whether it's the speaking industry or another target niche, what would you like those people thinking and saying about you five years from today?

Then, your next step, after you've written all those, is to boil that down to one little paragraph that summarizes all of those statements so that that gives you focus as to how you want to be known. You just go out there and earn that reputation, deserve to have that said and thought about you. Now, you also need to determine who you want to know you. So, be as clear as you can on the focus of what market you're going after. But, how do you get known in the speaking business? Well, first off, get active. Second, get a good idea of how you want to be known. And then third, take a close look at who you would like to know about you. As you do that your career will grow.

LESSON 54

HOW TO DO A WEBINAR, SPEAKING ON LINE

More and more often we are communicating from our laptops, iPads and smartphones. In fact, many of our audience members are only available via those virtual connections. How do you communicate differently when you're the speaker and the setting is a camera on your computer? What if the meeting is a hybrid with both an in-person audience and an online audience?

The easy answer is...you communicate truthfully. Be authentic. It's just you and the one other person on the receiving end of the connection.

In most cases there are no groups watching podcasts, webinars or on-screen collaborations. The more natural you can be the better. So, treat it as if you were in a live face-to-face meeting in the same room with your listeners.

Before the broadcast be sure to become familiar with your tools, the screen, the controls, the note taking and the question-and-answer processes. These vary from one system to the next. Once you're comfortable with the actions on your end then you can focus on your message and the needs of your audience. Also get a colleague to help you check what things look and sound like from the other end.

Call them and check your camera placement, the lighting on your face, the sound levels and any distractions that can be eliminated in advance.

Once the meeting begins, start right away. Assume that the spotlight is on, and everyone is watching you. Even if they aren't yet. Just greet the group, ask for responses to get them engaged and begin delivering your message. Have someone help you with late arrivals and mute the sounds made when they connect. In fact, you might want to mute all audience members until you are ready for them to interact with you live.

It is usually helpful to give instructions at the opening of the webinar about the mute button, background sounds or video distractions, and any of the key tools they will use. Also tell them what you will be sending to them or posting for download. That may eliminate some unnecessary questions or interruptions. Focus on your message. Say what you came to say and then interact with the folks as naturally as you can. You'll do well. Have fun with it.

THE SPEAKER'S PROFESSIONAL PLEDGE™

Based on what thousands of meeting planners have told me over my career, I created this document to assure them that I will do what they want me to do and not do what they don't want me to do.

I send this to my clients each time I am booked for a speaking engagement. You may use this as a checklist, even as a non-paid speaker, to assure that you are truly focused on providing value at the events where you speak.

Here is what I will do when I speak for you
by Jim Cathcart, CSP, CPAE

IN PREPARATION, I WILL

Be available to discuss plans for my speech.

Know what your organization does and why it does it.

Know why I am there and have a specific plan to accomplish your goals for my presentation.

Know the theme of your meeting and relate my presentation to it.

Know why your people would want to hear what I have to say on this topic.

Coordinate with other speakers or the speaker's bureau to assure your goals are met.

Notify you in advance of my travel itinerary or coordinate with your virtual platform.

ON-SITE, I WILL

Notify you when I arrive on site and contact you immediately should any serious delays occur.

Be accessible to you from the time I arrive until I leave.

Tell you the truth 100% of the time.

Retire early the night before my speech.

Be reasonable and considerate in my use of room charges and incidental expenses.

Be in the meeting room for a sound check at least one hour before I speak.

Be logged in on your virtual platform at least 30 minutes before my presentation.

Coordinate with the set-up crew and other presenters to make sure my needs fit your overall needs.

Stay out of the way until it is my turn to speak.

Study your audience and the other speakers to align my message with them.

Be dressed appropriately, always one-step more formal or business-like than the audience.

Provide an easy, brief introduction and be available to coach my introducer.

Make suggestions to the crew as to how to maximize audience impact through creative use of lights, sound or staging.

Be in the room, seated and visible to you even before my introduction begins.

Send you the files of any handouts or visuals I will be using.

DURING MY PRESENTATION, I WILL

Walk on stage cheerfully and open my speech with energy and purpose.

Never use off-color language or material.

Interact constantly with the audience and involve them through questions, a show of hands, eye contact and exercises as appropriate.

Present well-researched, profound information.

Use stories and humor liberally.

Use appropriate slides and audio clips or video clips to enhance the look, feel and impact of my speech.

React maturely, good-naturedly and flexibly to any problems that arise. This includes audio-visuals, lights, sounds, emergencies, etc.

Never be rude to an audience member.

Allow for questions and comments from the audience during my presentation.

Summarize my points and give ways to remember my key points.

Relate my points to your organization and people.

Never abuse my assignment by turning my speech into a sales pitch.

Only offer my books and services if approved or requested in advance.

Stick to my time frame and adjust if needed.

AFTER MY PRESENTATION, I WILL

Stay around after my speech briefly to answer questions, pose for photos, autograph books and hear audience comments.

Check out and depart with minimal effort to you.

Itemize my expenses if needed and bill you promptly after the speech. Provide receipts for larger expenses.

Promptly fill any orders for my products and services.

Send a PDF copy of my slides for you to distribute to each audience member as a follow-up, if desired.

Discuss strategies with you to continue the impact of my message during follow-up.

Never disclose any sensitive information about your organization.

Be willing to accept personal phone calls to follow up on the speech from individual audience members or executives.

IN SUMMARY

I will deliver an exceptionally good presentation in a highly professional manner.

©2023 Cathcart Institute

EPILOGUE

So, what did you think? Did we deliver on our promise to permanently alter your views toward public speaking? What surprised you? What helped you feel more confident as you face future presentations and speeches?

These tips, ideas and strategies did not come from me alone. They are the accumulated wisdom from the hundreds of top professionals and masterful speakers I've known. With thousands of hours spent both on convention stages and in the audiences I have seen it all! The smart, the silly and the ridiculous.

There were lessons there and I've endeavored to share them here with you.

Now, you're up! You are the Speaker.

Quick question: What will you be focused on?

Please answer, "On assuring that the value of my message reaches my audience." Thank you.

When you speak to an audience you are addressing many. But as they hear you, they hear just one...you. Be the person they hope you are.

Think specifically of delivering value that they can use. Tell them, "What this means to you is..."

Consider me now as your personal speech Mentor. Follow me on social media, comment on my posts, offer feedback on your experience with the ideas. Stay engaged. My personal mission is to help others live more abundantly. I sincerely hope I have done so for you.

In the Spirit of Growth,

Since 1977, Jim Cathcart has been helping people grow and succeed by bringing them mentorship, insights, resources, and skill development. Mr. Cathcart is a Mentor to Experts and Entrepreneurs and is one of the world's most award-winning professional speakers and authors. He travels the world delivering seminars and keynote speeches, as well as serving on corporate boards, university faculties or as a personal advisor to many senior executives and entrepreneurs.

The Experts Academy™ Mentorship

Each year Jim Cathcart guides a select group of successful achievers to the Top 1% of their chosen field. This results in them becoming *Certified Professional Experts, CPE™s.*

To be considered for this program contact us today. Includes monthly video meetings, personal & speech coaching, a Mastermind Summit, potentially authoring or coauthoring a published book, marketing and sales strategies, and plenty of facetime directly with Jim Cathcart.

https://cathcart.com/experts

Let's discover how much more successful you can be!

The Going Pro® Experience (3 month) Mentorship

When you are ready to truly commit to reaching the next levels of success, this is the program for you. Through weekly video meetings directly with Jim Cathcart you are guided to laser clarity on what you want and how to achieve it. Self-study video materials are provided along with direct coaching from Jim. An in-person Mastermind Retreat is included. The focus is on the monetization of your greatest natural abilities and most accessible resources.

https://cathcart.com/goingpro

More about Cathcart Institute

Cathcart.com is our primary website. It contains
articles, resources, videos, and recordings that are free for you
to download plus links to Jim's award-winning books, assessments,
recordings, and training materials.
For any needs that aren't met by the posted resources, simply give us a call or
drop us an e-mail at info@cathcart.com.

For scheduling speeches, interviews, appearances, consultations: Contact us at
Cathcart Institute, LLC.
Executive Office Austin, TX, USA

Phone: 1-805-777-3477
Website: https://cathcart.com E-mail: Info@cathcart.com

On social media, or Wikipedia simply search for
"Jim Cathcart" or "Cathcart Institute."

For Jim Cathcart's many books go to
Amazon.com, Barnes&Noble.com or your favorite bookstore.

For speaking engagements, contact us directly or through your favorite
speakers bureau.

COAUTHOR'S LETTER:

FROM JAN PAYNE

When Jim Cathcart, CSP, CPAE, asked me to write something for the author's page, the first thing that came to mind was gratitude. In 2009, I was introduced to Mr. Cathcart at an event where he was a Keynote Speaker. It was clearly one of the most impactful speeches I had ever heard. I stepped out of my comfort zone and went to the back of the room to tell him how amazing he was, how I felt he was speaking just to me, and how much of an impact his words had. He was kind enough to let me have a picture taken with him. When I came home from that event, I added this photo to my vision board. My goal at that time was, and still is to work with this talented man.

Vision boards work!

In 2014, I received an email from Jim Cathcart. OMG – are you kidding me? Would I like to help him with The Self-Motivation Handbook? Immediately I answered…let me think…YES!! I took the opportunity and had the most fun and challenging time working with him.

On Tuesday, April 19, 2016, I received an email from Jim!

I've written yet another book, this one is about speaking. The Title is "You're the Speaker™" Subtitle is: The Cathcart Method for Confident Communication in Public Speaking and Leading Meetngs. I'll send you an edit link so you can explore the Google Doc of it. Would you be interested in helping me to edit and complete that book? I can hire you as my editor or include you as my collaborator.

Would I be interested? YES!! The rest is history, well not quite!

I was in the middle of chemo (cancer treatment) in 2019, when I received the copies of this book. It was a hard-cover 2 volume edition, written in 2 languages! English and Chinese! I thought, at the time that was the most amazing feeling ever. It got even better. Jim Cathcart told me he was going to be in Denver, at the Gaylord Hotel for a speakers convention and asked if I could meet him for coffee.

Having been a part of the personal development industry for over 25 years, this has been the highlight of my career.

Currently, my new passion is neuroscience. I am a mental fitness coach and part of the Positive Intelligence community. You can take the assessment Assessments | Positive Intelligence and find out more on my website https://www.attractingpossibilities.com/courses/mental-fitness/

To your success, With much gratitude, Jan

ACKNOWLEDGMENTS

Who you are today reflects those who have come into your life over time. We carry these imprints long after we are aware of their influence.

The author would like to acknowledge the following group of amazing people who have helped to mold him into the speaker and person he is today. Their influence is not forgotten.

Harold Gash, Joe D. Willard, Tony Alessandra, Carol James, Mary Nixon, Marsha Field, Rick Little, Gary Goranson, Mark Victor Hansen, Keith DeGreen, Paula Cathcart, Jim Cathcart Jr.,

Terrence McCann (former executive director of Toastmasters International), Bill Johnson (former executive director of The National Speakers Association), Earl Nightingale, Zig Ziglar, Don Hutson, Denis Waitley, Joel Weldon, Jeanne Robertson, Robert Mayer Evans, Dr. David Chu, Roger Dawson, Bill Brooks, Bill Gove, Jim Newman, Patricia Fripp, Leo Hart, Jim Tunney, Spencer Johnson, Wendy Keller, John Buck, Don Varnadore, Matthew Pollard, Jimmie Haskell, Harold Payne, Daniel Burrus, Dr. Ken Druck, Marguerite Metcalf, Dennis Madden, Rodger Bland, Carolyn Brown Moore, Daniel Rex, Nancy McGraw, Amy Commans, and Alex Cuilty plus the many members of Speakers Roundtable over the 29 years of Jim's involvement with them.

There have been scores of other friends and colleagues as well, but that would turn this page into a membership directory of many volumes. Thank you all.

A special thank you to Jan Payne and Maureen Richmond for their expert help with this manuscript, and to Michael D. Butler for bringing the book to a reality through his publishing expertise.

THE CATHCART METHOD™

What is "The Cathcart Method™"?

Jim Cathcart's personal style and approach to public speaking is a very natural and thoughtful one. His belief is that your greatest strength is found in your natural abilities, not in some magical formula you learned and rehearsed. People tell Jim that his sincerity comes across strongly. They trust him. They can tell that he is telling the truth.

This is a way to Be, Do and Have what you want. This is not a course design, but rather it is a description of the personal qualities you will want to cultivate in yourself as a speaker.
The formula for this method is "FIRST PAGE."
This is your memory tool for the key elements to this method.

F.I.R.S.T.

    F - Flexible – be able to change quickly without losing control

    I – Intentional – make everything happen for a reason

    R- Real – don't fake it or you won't really make it

    S- Sincere – tell the truth, be yourself

    T- Thoughtful *(and Considerate)*

P.A.G.E.

    P- Playful – make this fun for everyone

    A- Appropriate *(and Professional)*

    G- Grateful – express your appreciation openly

    E- Enthusiastic – bring energy, don't expect to receive it from others

When you cultivate these qualities in yourself you will increase your natural magnetism and your ability to deliver any message with confidence and impact. What has set Jim Cathcart apart as a presenter and caused so many of his mega-successful colleagues to follow his example and hire him to speak to their groups is The Cathcart Method™. This is not just a skillset; it is a new and more authentic way of being that allows you to be the most powerful person you can be...You!

The Cathcart Method™
See it done, Think it through, Notice more, Make it you.

"FIRST PAGE"
Be: Flexible, Intentional, Real, Sincere, Thoughtful,
Playful, Appropriate, Grateful and Enthusiastic

See it done
Think it through. Learn how and why it works. Discuss it.
Notice more. See it done again.
Make it you. Always apply this learning to your next speech.
The combination of examples, experience and reflection is essential.
You will never again be as anxious or intimidated about speaking. Your thinking about yourself as a speaker will shift permanently!
Make it you! By applying **The Cathcart Method**™ from What to do when You're The Speaker™: You can develop the same poise and confidence that you see in professional speakers and media personalities. It is a learnable craft, and this program is your key to the behind-the-scenes thinking, strategies and skills it takes to master it. Let Jim Cathcart be your speaking and communication mentor.

For in-person training programs, keynote speeches, or individual coaching go to http://cathcart.com. Jim is often retained by executives and celebrities as their speaking Mentor. Our goal is to help **you** develop the confidence and skill to become a Professional Expert and a Master Communicator.

Going Pro®: Are you ready to begin speaking for a fee? Please contact us about personal guidance to advance your career in speaking. By now, you already know Jim Cathcart's credentials as he has trained many of today's top Hall of Fame pros. We have a wealth of resources and experts who can help you identify your best topics, develop your platform mastery, create learning materials, write a book and get it published, and refine your brand as a professional speaker and expert.

Website http://Cathcart.com/goingpro

See it done, Think it through, Notice more, Make it you.

Here are some of the concepts Jim lives and teaches. This is evident in his "method" or personal style. For more on these concepts access Jim's many books, videos and courses online and in bookstores, or join The Experts Academy™.

Become an Expert in your field, The Top 1%
Think Like A Start Up™ – Like An Owner
Fully Commit or Don't Play
Think like your Recipient, not just as the Provider
Have Fun or Find A New Game
Suspend Your Selfish Interests
Focus On Providing Value
Consider Each Step A Beginning
Become Excellent At Gratitude
Learn Intelligent Observation
Learn Pattern Interruption
Practice Incremental Enhancement
Develop Habitual Initiative
Master Reputation Creation
Just Tell The Truth
Discover Your Patterns – Systematic Inspection
Become a Skilled Problem Solver

Know What You Are Paid To Do

Know Your "Real ESTATE"

Manage your Causation Chain™

Achieve "Escape Velocity" Often

Do Your Homework

Read The Owner's Manuals

Meet The Parents

Act While The Impulse Is There (positive acts only)

Capture Your Power Minutes™

Know What To Wonder About

Be Great At Expressing What You Want

Listen Like You Want To Understand More

Handle Your Relationships Intentionally

Do The First Step

Ask The Daily Question

Do It Now!

Assume You Could Be Wrong

Increase Intentionality

Never Stop Improving

Other works by Jim Cathcart include:

- » Mentor Minutes, Reach the Top 1% of Any Field, (Cathcart Press/Beyond Publishing, 2023)
- » Professional Growth: Acorns to Oak Trees, 16 lessons on Video (TomeApp.com Publisher,2023)
- » HI-REV for Small Business by Dennis Madden and Jim Cathcart (Beyond Publishing, 2022)
- » Intelligent Curiosity by Jim Cathcart with Lisa Patrick (Beyond Publishing, 2021)
- » The Relationship Intelligence® Advanced Certification (online course) by Mentored.com
- » You Are The Speaker (World Masters Press 2019) in English and Mandarin Chinese
- » The Sales IQ Plus™ online assessment, coauthored with Jeffrey Gitomer and Tony Alessandra, (Assessments24x7.com, 2015),
- » Relationship Selling: The Eight Competencies of Top Sales Producers (Cathcart Institute, 2015)
- » Confident Communication: Public Speaking and Leading Meetings DVD/CD (Cathcart Institute, 2009)
- » 8 eBooks in the Relationship Selling series:
- » Introduction to Relationship Selling (Acanthus, 2006)
- » Sales Readiness: How Preparation Leads to Opportunity (Acanthus, 2006)
- » Finding the Buyers (Acanthus, 2007)
- » Connecting with Your Customer (Acanthus, 2007)
- » Sales Psychology: Understanding the Mind of the Buyer (Acanthus, 2007)
- » Sales Presentations (Acanthus, 2008)
- » Getting the Sale: Confirming the Commitment to Buy (Acanthus, 2008)
- » Customer Loyalty (Acanthus, 2007)
- » The Eight Competencies of Relationship Selling (Leading Authorities Press 2002)
- » The Acorn Principle (St. Martin's Press, 1998, 1999, 2000, Revised 2015)
- » Inspiring Others to Win (Griffin, 1998)

- » The Professional Speaker™ Business System & Learning Library (Professional Speaking Institute, 1997 audio and video)
- » The Sales Professional's Idea-A-Day Guide (Dartnell, 1996)
- » The Winning Spirit (Griffin, 1996)
- » Speaking Secrets of the Masters (Speakers Roundtable, 1995)
- » The Acorn Principle (Cathcart Institute, 1995 Audio Album)
- » Rethinking Yourself (Cathcart Institute, 1993, Video)
- » Be Your Own Sales Manager (Simon & Schuster/Fireside Books, 1990)
- » Relationship Selling (Perigee/Putnam, 1990)
- » Insights into Excellence (Executive Books, 1988-90)
- » Selling by Objectives (Prentice Hall, 1988)
- » Win Through Relationships (Nightingale-Conant, 1988, video)
- » Think Service (Universal Video, 1987)
- » Meeting with Success (Nightingale-Conant, 1987, audio album)
- » Helping People Grow (Levitz-Sommer Video, 1986, video)
- » Superstar Selling (Nightingale-Conant, 1986, audio album)
- » The Business of Selling (Prentice Hall, 1985)
- » Relationship Strategies (Nightingale-Conant, 1984, audio album)
- » Communication Dynamics (US Jaycees, 1976)

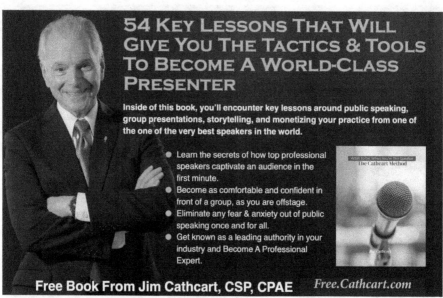

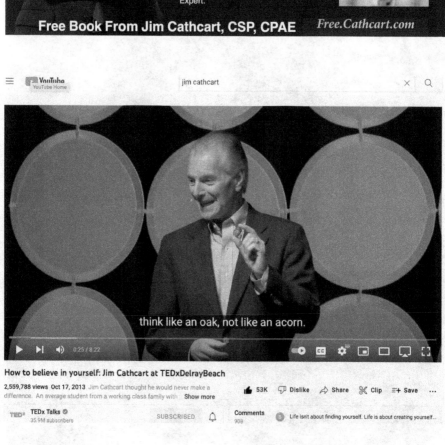

CPSIA information can be obtained
at www.ICGtesting.com
Printed in the USA
BVHW05093825052 3
664859BV00003B/161